FROM **LEVEL HILL**

TO **CAPITOL HILL**

Frank Bates

Decatur, GA

From Level Hill to Capitol Hill
Copyright 2014 Frank Bates

Address inquiries to the publisher: Mister Sammy Pulishing

ISBN: 978-0-692-24213-1
LCCN: 2014914631

First Printing: September 2014
Printed in the United States of America

Composed and edited by Allwrite Communications Inc.

Dedication

*This book is dedicated to a very dear and respected friend
who was my mentor and school teacher, the late Calvin G.
Turner. Other than my parents, I credit Mr. Turner for setting
me on my path to whatever success that I may have achieved.
It was Mr. Turner who suggested to Mr. Willie Bolton, of Dr.
Martin Luther King Jr.'s field staff, that I be put in charge
of the students who were the foot soldiers of the Civil Rights
Movement in Crawfordville, Georgia, during that long hot
summer of 1965.*

*Calvin was the first black man that I knew of to openly and
publicly opposed white people and denounced segregation
in Taliaferro County. This was done before the passage of the
Civil Rights and Voting Rights Acts, at a time when it was very
detrimental and, sometimes, fatal for black people to oppose
white people in the South. Calvin put his and his family's life
in jeopardy because of his direct opposition to segregation and
injustice in Taliaferro County.*

*In my opinion, every black person in Taliaferro and sur-
rounding counties owe a debt of gratitude to a man that gave
so much to bring about social change and equality to so many.
Mr. Turner, may your soul rest in peace as a reward for
your sacrifice and dedication to mankind.*

Dedication

Table of Contents

Acknowledgements

I want to acknowledge those brave and courageous students, too many to name, who walked out of the Murden High School on that hot morning of May 28, 1965, to protest the firing of our five black teachers. As you read this book, you can take great pride in telling your children and grandchildren that you were there and you took part in making a difference in this country. You were the foot soldiers of the Civil Rights Movement in Crawfordville. Your bravery and dedication to equality and social change will never be forgotten. The actions of those young students lead to ground-breaking and land- mark decisions in this country. I am honored to have been a part of such a heroic and committed group of students.

CHAPTER 1

Growing Up in Crawfordville

I was born on December 22, 1947, to the late James Thomas
Bates, Jr., and Mary Bertha Bates in Taliaferro County,
Georgia. Crawfordville is the county seat, but we lived out
in the country in the Level Hill community about three miles
down a dirt road.

In 1947, Jackie Robinson was the first black major league
baseball player with the Brooklyn Dodgers. There were approximately 9,000 TV sets in this country with about 139 TV sta-
tions. The Cardinals defeated the Eagles 28-21 to win the NFL
championship. The New York Yankees won the World Series
in the final game against the Brooklyn Dodgers. Philadelphia
beat Chicago to win the NBA title. A new house cost $12,309,
car $1,500, gas $0.18 per gallon, and bread $0.12 per loaf. The
average annual income was $2,854, which was somewhat de-
ceptive because many families in my community would have
been overjoyed if they could have earned $2,850 a year.

I am the youngest of seven children: six boys and one girl.
Big families were the order of the day back then because that
meant that my father didn't have to hire anyone to help us
to work the fields and gather the crops. He probably couldn't

afford to hire anyone any way. We were a little more fortunate than some of the families in our community because our grandfather had the foresight and the opportunity to purchase 100 acres of land in the early 1900s. He could not pay for it, though, so he moved to New York and worked as a longshoreman on the docks to earn enough money to pay for the land while my father, grandmother, and a dear lady to the family, Ms. Lula Peek, maintained the farm. After working in New York for three years, he had saved enough money to pay off the note at the bank in Crawfordville. Then he came back home to work on the farm. When, in later years, another 100 acres came available, he pledged the first 100 acres against the second 100 acres as collateral. He knew how important it was to own land, so he eventually bought another 57 acres. Those 257 acres of land have been in our family for three generations now. I believe I have been over every inch of that land when we were farming.

Our work day on the farm would start around 5 a.m. and end around 8 p.m., or whenever it got dark outside. My Daddy believed in working from sun up to sundown. My brother Howard told the story about the first time Daddy allowed him to go up to Cincinnati to work with our uncle in the construction industry one summer after they had "laid by" the cotton. That meant we had finished plowing the cotton and doing all that we could do, and now we were just waiting until the cotton opened so we could pick it. It usually took about two to three weeks for the cotton to open. Howard said that the foreman came around that first day around 5 o'clock, announcing, "Okay guys, it's time to go."

Howard asked our uncle, "Where are we going?"

He responded, "It's time to go, home boy."

"But the sun is still way up yonder."

"We don't work by the sun up here, you fool. We work by the hour."

Howard could not believe that people quit working, as he described it, "in the middle of the day." He had been used to working until it was dark. That day, Howard said that he earned $13, the most money he had ever earned in one day. He wrote home and sent his check stub to show how much money he had earned and told our mother that he didn't want to come back home. Eventually, he did come back home that year to help Daddy gather the crops, but as soon as they were gathered, he went back to Cincinnati, where he has been since 1952.

Land at the time was approximately $25 per acre. Cotton was the cash crop, meaning that the only source of income for us was from the cotton. Once it was picked and taken to the "gin house," which was where the process of separating the seeds from the cotton fibers took place. We started picking cotton around the latter part of August or the first of September and finished around the latter part of October. It took approximately 1,500 pounds of cotton with the seeds in it to make a 500-pound bale, which was the average size of a bale of cotton once it was ginned. The average amount of money generated from a bale of cotton was about $500, or $1 per pound. We had about 20 acres of cotton, and we would make approximately 20 bales of cotton in a good year.

The gin house in our area of Taliaferro County was in a little town called Hillman. Wyman Dozier owned the Cotton Gin and the General Store. Hillman was a thriving community at one time with three businesses: a post office, the train depot photo tent, and a hotel with 50 rooms. The hotel burned down many years ago and was never rebuilt. The little community was named in the honor of Andrew Lafayette Hillman, who was a mineralogist. He purchased the 2,700 acres of land in 1885, and Hillman, Georgia, was incorporated as a town on October 22, 1887, by an act of the Georgia General Assembly.

In later years, the only things remaining in Hillman were the Depot, one General Store and the Cotton Gin, along with many loyal dedicated families. My sister-in-law, Sadie Smith, and her family lived in the Hillman Community. Mr. Wyman, as he was called, owned the general store, and he sold everything that we needed, such as, shoes, clothes, food, all farming equipment, fertilizer, seeds, gas, oil, coals, kerosene, and anything else that you could name.

We loved going down to Hillman when we were children so we could get a cold drink of Nehi or a Double Cola and a slice of hoop cheese. Most of all, we enjoyed getting two cookies for a penny.

All during the year, my father and all of the other farmers in the community would establish credit with Mr. Wyman. When we needed something, we would go to Hillman and credit it. Mr. Wyman would record what we owed on a ticket, then put it in a drawer, and hold the ticket until harvest time. The term used throughout the rural South for paying your bills at the end of the year was "settle up."

When we picked and ginned the cotton at Mr. Wyman's Cotton Gin, he would tell my father how much money he could pay him per pound for the cotton. My father, along with all of the other farmers, did not have the option of negotiating the price per pound. They had to take what was offered. The farmers felt that the price that Mr. Wyman offered was fair.

My grandfather would say that Mr. Wyman was a "fair man" toward "colored" people. In fact, I think that was the accepted view of most colored people in the community at that time.

Daddy would go to Mr. Wyman to settle up. Mr. Wyman would be the only one keeping records for the items and the amount of money we owed. This process was not just the way he did business; this was the way it was done throughout the rural South during the late 40s and early 50s. Black folks could not nor would they dispute a bill that the white man said they owed. Disputing or challenging the white man during those days was viewed as being "uppity," and you probably would not have credit extended to you anymore. Without credit, the farms could not make it through the next year to harvest time.

During the fall was harvest time, but we called that period of the year "cotton picking time" because that was when the cotton was picked, taken to the gin house, and then sold. After farming for a full year and the cotton was picked and sold, that was the only time farmers received any money. Getting paid once a year is difficult to understand or visualize for most people today, for these days, people have difficulty making it from one week to the next.

During the late 40s and early 50s, which was my child-hood years, families were very resourceful, and they made do. "Making do" is a term that was used throughout the South, especially among the black people, which simply means instead of buying a new item, just fix the old one or simply do without.

My father had a fourth grade education and my mother had a third grade education, but they were the smartest people I knew because they reared seven children, cultivated 20 acres of cotton, and kept a roof over our heads. They clothed us adequately and had plenty of food for us all the time. I cannot ever remember going hungry, in fact. It may not have been what we wanted to eat, but we did not go hungry.

Although the farmers only got money during harvest time, my father used to sell and distribute moonshine throughout the year. Moonshine is the term for the illegal manufacturing of corn liquor because the liquor was made during the night in the woods, where the only light was from the moon shinning. Other names for this liquor included "white lightning" and "stump run" because people use to sit around on tree stumps while waiting for the liquor to be made. Another name is "corn liquor" because corn is one of the main ingredients used in the manufacturing of this illegal liquor.

My father got involved in the sale and distribution of liquor when he was a young man. Down through the years, every one of my brothers, including me, helped him with the distribution of liquor until his death in 1964. The selling moonshine gave my father a little more extra income for the family. I grew up around moonshine, for drinking moonshine was very common in the rural South.

I used to go with my father sometimes on Friday evenings down to Mr. Pete and Mrs. Fannie Brinkley's house. Ms. Fannie use to have fish fries on Friday nights, and people in the neighborhood would go for some good times, such as platting the "May Pole" to live music from guitars and harmonicas, and buck dancing. Ms. Fannie did not have electric lights like many other families, so she used kerosene lamps as the source of light. Black folks did not have much money, but they always found ways to have fun and enjoy themselves. I used to think these men were having the best time drinking corn liquor, buck dancing and picking guitars. I use to say, "Boy, I cannot wait until I get big so I could go down to Ms. Fannie and have a good time."

One of the men in the community named Jack Moore would pick his guitar and sing songs titled "*Early One Morning All I had was Gone*" and "*Corina, Corina*." This is what we called "low down dirty blues." black folks have always used music to express their feelings – even during the slavery period. They used their songs, music and dance as a form of entertainment and expression even though times were very hard socially and economically. They used every resource they had just to scratch out a living for their families. I don't mean to infer that it was only black folks working hard and trying to make a living, there were white folks working just as hard to support their families as well. Most blacks worked either on a farm, saw mill, in the pulp wood business, or domestic work. There was only one garment factory in Crawfordville, but only white people were allowed to work there.

We had jobs and chores as early as I can remember. My brother Horace said when he was 3 years old, his "first job was to keep the chickens off the front porch." I do not know that to be a fact because he was the oldest brother and there is no one around who can dispute it. Plus, Horace has been known to talk a lot and stretch the truth. My sister, Dorothy, and I really did have jobs, though. Dorothy was responsible for getting wood for the stove so my mother could cook. I was responsible for getting the firewood for heating the house. We were also responsible for bringing in the chambers ("slop jars") every evening and taking them out every morning. Like our clothes, our chores, such as bringing in the chambers, were passed down as we got older. Thus, everyone would have the same responsibilities at one point or another.

As we got older, we assumed more jobs and responsibilities. We planted 20 acres of cotton, and it was very important to my father to get the cotton picked as quickly as he could and as inexpensively as he could. When I was about 8 or 9 years old, my father used to require me to pick at least 50 pounds of cotton per day, and as I got older, he required that I pick 100 pounds per day. Later, his requirement was 200 pounds a day. He used to say to my brother Charles, "If you don't pick 200 pounds today, you don't go to school the next day." That was a great incentive for us not to play around because we wanted to go to school, not because we loved school so much, rather we did not want to stay home and pick cotton all day. Anyone who grew up on a farm during that era can attest that farm life was tough and hard.

When I would tell people how many siblings I have, almost always, they would say that I know that she was spoiled being the only girl out of six boys. They just didn't know my daddy, though. He did not spoil anyone. All of us had to work and carry our own weight.

Birthdays were never important to us back then, and we never had a birthday party or recognized our birthday in any way. My daddy was not about to stop or let us take off because of a birthday. My birthday is December 22, and my mother would cook two cakes for the Christmas holiday. She would say, "One of these cakes is for your birthday." Still, we couldn't cut either of them until Christmas. I think those cakes were really for the Christmas season, but she would just say one of the cakes was mine. My family was no different from all of the other families in our community. Birthdays were not a big deal, and the girls in the families had to work in the fields just like the boys.

Growing up on that farm was not all bad because what my parents taught me and what I learned has stayed with me to this very day and has proven to be valuable in my adult life. Some of the significant traits that my parents instilled in all of my brothers and my sister included accepting responsibility; the willingness to work to earn my own way; and most of all, respect and discipline.

CHAPTER 2

STARTING SCHOOL

In September of 1953, I followed the footsteps of my brothers and sister by enrolling in school at the Level Hill Elementary School, which was a one-room building on the same grounds as our church, Level Hill Baptist Church. One teacher taught everyone from the first through the fourth grade. After completing the fourth grade, students would go to school in town at Murden Elementary and High School.

There were probably six or seven schools in Taliaferro County. Typical at the time, almost every church community had its own one- or two-room school. It was amazing how the one teacher was able to keep discipline and instruction going at the same time for students of varying age and ability. There were four tables arranged in the one room where each grade level sat at separate tables. Ms. Bird was my first grade teacher, but she left shortly after I started school. Ms. Annie B. Moore from the Springfield Community in Hancock County came in to finish out the school term. Ms. Moore was a younger teacher who was tall and slender with long black hair. Bottom line, she was very pretty. I visited her in 2010 shortly before her death. I also had the pleasure of attending and speaking at her retirement celebration in Hancock County after teaching for over 30 years in the public school system.

I have distinct and fond memories of my first year in school at that one-room school, which will remain with me for a lifetime. School started at 8 a.m., and we had a little recess from 10:00 to 10:30 a.m. Then we had big recess and lunch at 12:00 to 1:00 before school ended at 3:00 p.m. Back then, the school did not have any toys or equipment for children to play with, so we had to be creative in our school yard activities and games. There was a very popular game that boys and girls played together called "Popping the Whip." Dodge ball was another game that boys and girls played together. However, there were certain games that only boys played called "Rabbit and Dog." One group of boys would be the rabbit, and another group of boys would be the dogs. The object of the game was for the dogs to catch the rabbit. The boys who were rabbits would go down through the woods running, and about five minutes later, the boys who were in the dog group would start chasing the rabbit, barking like dogs. "Horse and Buggy" and "Little Sally Walker" were popular games for girls. Boys would climb a small tree almost to the top until it would start bending, and then we would ride it down to the ground. I know the games would seem stupid to children now, but they were fun to us.

My first grade book was titled "Bob and Jane," and some of the books were titled "Dick and Jane." They had a blue back, and some of them had red backs. We used only second-hand books. In fact, I cannot remember us ever having new books at Level Hill. Approximately, 30 or 35 children would be in school on a given day. More children would be in school during the winter months because during the summer and fall of the year children had to help with the planting and plowing of the crops and other farm duties.

Level Hill Baptist Church was a second Sunday church, which means that we only held church services once per month on the second Sunday. All of the churches in the black communities, back then, only held church services once per month, but Sunday school was every Sunday. We were expected to go to Sunday school every Sunday.

The church was a place where we could come together and see other family members and friends. After the church service was over, we would stand around the church grounds for another hour or two catching up on what was going on in each other's lives. I remember my dress suit; of course, it was not bought for me. I think that brown double-breasted, pinstripe suit was bought for one of my older brothers, and it was passed down to me. You may wonder how could a suit last that long. Well, you have to understand that it was only worn once a month on the second Sunday, and as soon as we got home from church, it was understood that the first thing you did was to pull off those "Sunday clothes" and hang them up until next month.

Another event that people looked forward to was the "Spreading of Dinner." This was an occasion when each family would prepare a box of food, bring it to the church, and spread it out on the tables on the church grounds. My mother would always leave something in her box for our family. This was a time every one ate well. This was one big community eating and fellowshipping together.

Our pastor, at that time, was Reverend Carter from Atlanta. After church service before he went back to Atlanta, he would have dinner with various members of the church. When it came our time to have the pastor for dinner, the children had to wait until the preacher finished eating before we could eat. Many times, the preacher would sit at the table after he finished eating a half hour or more just talking and smoking cigars. We would be praying that he would hurry up and leave the dining room so we could eat our dinner. It was considered ill-mannered for children to talk while grown folks were talking. Daddy did not have to say a word. He would give you *that* look to let you know that grown folks are talking and you better shut up or move away from around them.

There are many memories that I have about my life and growing up in rural Georgia around Level Hill. Discipline, respect and hard work were the norm. Child abuse was a term that did not exist back then because if it had, my father and mother would be just getting out of the chain gang because they did not "spare the rod." My daddy would pull a limb off a tree or pull up a cotton stalk and beat us all over the body and dare us to cry. If we did, he would say, "Dry it up." I know that my parents loved us, and I appreciate their discipline now. Lord, back then, though, I thought it was the worst thing in the world.

We all looked forward to the time leading up to the second week of August. We would lay by the crops, which meant that we would have plowed the crops for the last time, and were waiting for the cotton bows to open for picking. This was a time for us to clean up around the church. Each family was expected to clean off their family graves, and dust and wash the church windows all in an effort to get ready for the "home coming." People who formerly lived in the Level Hill Community but had moved up North would come back home each second week in August for a family reunion and home coming at the church.

The second Sunday in August was a big day in the community when everyone was expected to be at church. Of course, we had the dreaded revival service that started on Monday and end on Friday night. All the children in the community were expected to attend revival service and sit on the front rows in the church. Those benches were called the "mourner's bench." Traditionally, church members would pray on the mourner's bench for all the sinners, hoping they would feel the Spirit, join the church, and ultimately be baptized the next month in September.

My brother Gordon and I joined the church during revival service in August 1959. After joining the church, I did not have to sit on the mourner's bench anymore. I have been a member of Level Hill Church ever since. When I am deceased, I expect to be buried in the family plot next to my mother and brother, Gordon.

CHAPTER 3

MURDEN ELEMENTARY AND HIGH SCHOOL

I n September of 1954, the Taliaferro County School System abolished all independent rural schools in the county. The doors on the one-room school at Level Hill were then closed forever. That school had served my five brothers, my sister, and both of my parents. Leaving Level Hill and going to Murden came with mixed emotions because I was leaving the friendly confines of a school where I knew everyone or was related to for a school where I did not know anyone and a teacher we all heard about named Mr. Teddleton (Ted).

Mr. Teddleton was a teacher everyone feared. The other teacher would send the students to Mr. Teddleton for punishment whenever someone misbehaved in class. He taught the 6th grade for about 15 or 20 years. Therefore, almost everyone who attended Murden was in Mr. Teddleton's class.

He had several straps that he used. Back in those days corporal punishment was permitted in school. I am not so sure whether that was the wrong thing to do by taking corporal punishment out of the schools, but I will leave that argument to those who know much more about that subject than I. Girls got a certain number of licks in their hand, and the boys either got their licks on their butt or sometimes in their hands. We dared not to come home complaining about getting a whipping at school from Mr. Teddleton because we would get another one from our father.

Ms. Kibble was my new second grade teacher at Murden. She retained me because she felt that I did not master second grade work. In retrospect, this was probably the best thing that could have happened to me because my new classmates and I have been friends until this very day. Two of those classmates continued on to Fort Valley State University with me: George Turner and Jo Ann Richardson.

Like most schools in the rural South, our school was small. There were approximately 100 students in high school. We did not have a baseball team or a football team, but we did have a girls and boys basketball team. All of our home games were played outdoors on dirt. We did not have a pavement or asphalt basketball court until 1962. Our superintendent, Ms. Lola Williams, authorized the paving of our basketball court, and it was a welcome venture. Just imagine trying to dribble a basketball on a dirt court. I am sure that many students would have dropped out of school if it had not been for the opportunity to play high school basketball. In fact, basketball played an important role in the lives of many students at our school because there were not very many school activities that really engaged the interest of the boys. Playing on the basketball team was something that almost every boy looked forward to back then.

Most of the predominately black schools in the surrounding counties did not have gymnasiums, but all of the white schools had gymnasiums. During this time, Georgia and most of the other Southern states were operating under the separate but equal doctrine. There was nothing equal about the black schools and the white schools other than they were built about the same time.

CHAPTER 4

OUR LONG HOT SUMMER OF 1965

As far back as I can remember, the summer of 1965 began as every other summer. The country had not healed from the death of President John F. Kennedy. Congress had just passed the all-important Voting Right Bill of 1965, and a year earlier, President Johnson signed the Civil Rights Bill of 1964 into law. These were some very important pieces of legislation. Like everyone else, I had been watching on TV and listening to the radio about all the Civil Rights activities that were taking place around the South. I had no particular interest other than admiring the courage of those involved in the various campaigns in Mississippi, Alabama and Atlanta. I used to read *Jet* magazine and watch TV about the Freedom Riders as they traveled across the South. I also watched the news about the three Civil Rights workers named Civil Rights workers named James Chaney, Michael Schwerner and Andrew Goodman who were missing in Mississippi. Every evening, I would watch the news about the march from Selman to Montgomery, Alabama. In May 1965, my life changed forever.

I was 17 years old in the 11th grade and was getting promoted to the 12th grade. It was the end of the school year. Calvin

Turner, one of our teachers, gave us the news that the superintendent, Lola Williams, had failed to renew the contracts of five of our prominent black teachers. These teachers had been teaching at Murden High School for a number of years. They were dedicated, committed and very interested in us learning and being the best that we could be.

Not only were they interested in the students, some of the teachers were involved in the community, helping the parents to learn how to read, write and count. Mr. Turner, our science teacher, was one of the teachers the superintendent failed to renew his contract. To my knowledge, she did not give a legitimate reason for not renewing their contracts.

Calvin Turner was a local teacher who grew up in Taliaferro County and attended public school there. His parents sent him to Boggs Academy in Swainsboro, Georgia, for high school. Boggs Academy was a prestigious private school for blacks during the 50s and 60s. After graduating from Boggs, Turner enrolled in Fort Valley State College, where he graduated and eventually came back to Taliaferro County to teach. He was the girls' basketball coach in the early 60s, and he put together one of the best girls team that Murden High School ever had. In 1964, our girls beat Southside High School in Comer, Georgia. Southside was the only school in our area that had a gym, and they had both a good boys and girls team every year.

Turner demanded much from those girls. I remember people saying that Mr. Turner was too hard on those girls, but as we found out later, that hard work really paid off in the end. That year, our girls went on to win the region and then went on to the state. They lost very narrowly to a well-coached and talented team from Roberta, Georgia.

Turner was very dedicated and compassionate about everything he under took, including his commitment to social change for blacks. During 1964 and 1965, he attended some of the Southern Christian Leadership Conferences (SCLC) workshops and had the pleasure of meeting Reverend Hosea Williams, one of Dr. Martin Luther King, Jr's lieutenants.

There were many issues regarding inequalities among the races that needed to be addressed in Taliaferro County during that time, but only one issue was raised during that time: the firing of our prominent black teachers. This was the catalyst that led to the largest civil rights campaign since Selma and Birmingham. We heard from a reliable source that the reason our superintendent refused to renew those teachers' contract was that she heard that those teachers were helping black folks to read and write so they could register to vote because the voting rights bill had just passed and signed into law.

Turner had quietly organized us and gave us the idea of protesting the firing of our black teachers by staging a walkout of the school. The word got around the school in a matter of hours. On May 28, 1965, when the buses brought the children to school that morning, we got off of the buses and refused to go inside the school building. We congregated outside where the buses usually parked. It was a very successful boycott. However, everyone did not participate, but for the most part, it was successful and captured the superintendent's attention and the powers to be.

There was no turning back after that. The local student movement was ignited, and it went on to capture the nation's attention. The students who had participated in the school boycott marched up Lexington Avenue to Friendship Baptist

Church. At the church, Willie Bolton, J. T. Johnson and several other Civil rights workers met us there. Bolton was the field secretary for Georgia's Southern Christian Leadership Conference (SCLC) organizer. He was mapping out our strategy for what we would do next. The civil rights workers were getting us fired up and motivated by introducing us to the freedom songs, such as *"I Ain't Gonna Let Nobody Turn Me Around," "I Love Everybody," "Which Side Are You On," "We Shall Overcome,"* and many more that were made popular during the Civil Rights Movement of the 60s.

Bolton and others talked to us about being nonviolent and that we would conduct ourselves in a nonviolent manner at all times. Being nonviolent, he explained, did not mean that we were afraid, but that we were willing to accept the worse. We had all seen and heard about what Dr. King had gone through in the Montgomery movement and how he was able to bring about equality and change through his nonviolent doctrine.

We all knew that black folks in Crawfordville, Georgia, did not have the same rights and privileges the white folks in Crawfordville had. Bolton led a peaceful march downtown and marched around the courthouse singing the freedom songs. Some of us made an attempt to go in the front of Bonner's Cafe to order something to eat. A white lady, Ann Lou Bonner, owned Bonner's Cafe. Before this date, no Black person had attempted to go in the front for service. There were seats in the back where the cooking was done for blacks to sit and eat. It was shocking to the white people sitting in there that day to see black folks coming in the front door for service. Of course, we were turned around and told to get out and we did. We did not create a scene and we did not agree with her. We came out of the door and Willie Bolton told us to sit on the steps in front of the door to create a sit-in. We sat down and started singing our songs, not allowing anyone else to enter the cafe. Bonner's Cafe was no different than all of the other white-owned cafes and eating establishments across the South at that time. Black folks worked as cooks and dish washers but could not eat up front.

The Sheriff, Milton Moore (Bo Moore), was called, and he came up and told us to leave the premises. If we did not leave, he would lock us up in jail. We were not afraid of going to jail, but we were not organized to go to jail. Thus, Willie instructed us to leave, so we marched back to Friendship Baptist Church in a peaceful nonviolent manner.

We wanted to bring pressure and attention to the powers that be that we were not pleased with the superintendent's firing of our black teachers without justification or a good cause. That night, we had a mass rally at Friendship Baptist Church to talk about what had happened that day and to plan our strategy for the next day. The decision was made that night to expand our interest and demands from wanting our teachers reinstated to wanting to use the only gymnasium in the county to play our home basketball games. The white students at Alexander H. Stephens High School had used the gym since it was built. There were two schools in Taliaferro County: Murden was for the blacks, and Alexander H. Stephens was for whites.

The name Murden came from a prominent, wealthy landowner named Henning Daniel Murden in the Robinson community of Taliaferro County. It is said that when one of his slaves left the plantation, after the emancipation of slaves, he was given a certain sum of money. The former slave took his money and bought 64 acres of land where Friendship Baptist

Church is now located and started a school for Blacks. The white school was named in honor of Alexander H. Stephens, the vice president of the Confederate States of America. His home was in Crawfordville, GA. The state park and museum is also named in his honor.

Our list of demands and interests now included: the right to register to vote without a hassle; the opportunity to go to the state park and swimming pool; the insistence that white store owners hire blacks; and blacks be hired to work in the courthouse other than as janitors and landscapers. The superintendent refused to meet with representatives from the black community to discuss the concerns, so we made the decision to boycott the white stores downtown, hoping the storeowners would talk to the superintendent and encourage her to meet with us. Still, she refused to meet with us regarding our concerns.

We started a selective buying campaign (boycott) of all of the white stores. We would march in a single-file line up and down the sidewalks all day with our signs asking people not to shop in these stores. Many black people in the county did not have transportation to go to the neighboring counties to shop, so we would organize carpools in an effort to get people rides to the stores in the neighboring counties. The boycott was very successful because every week we would see food being thrown out because no one was buying it. We learned, through this effort, that the white folks had been buying most of their groceries from the neighboring counties where the fruits and vegetables were fresh and cheaper. Blacks were buying most of the groceries from the stores in Crawfordville. Many stores would extend credit to the black people because many of them lived on a fixed income, and they only got money through public assistance or social security.

I do not mean to insinuate that almost everyone was on some form of public assistance because they were not. Most people worked, and some did not get paid every week. Therefore, they would credit their groceries until payday.

That particular year, 1965, the white students were not using the gym because they did not have enough students in school to have a basketball team. There were approximately 75 white students in grade eight (8) through twelve (12). We asked the superintendent to allow us to use the gym, which had been paid for with state and local taxes from whites and blacks. Instead, she resurfaced our outdoor basketball court with a fresh layer of asphalt. After a week of mass meetings, Bolton and the civil rights workers said that they had to go back to Atlanta for a few days, but they wanted to leave someone in charge of the students until they got back. Little did I know that was their strategy and way of turning the movement over to local control. Their job was to come, get the movement started, organize the blacks, and move on.

Turner suggested that I be left in charge of the student activities until they got back in a few days. I proudly took the role, hoping for a reprieve as soon as they got back. Well, that few days turned into a few weeks before they came back. By that time, I was well on my way to a leadership position with the movement, and the dedicated, brave students had accepted me as their leader. Our eyes were set on integrating the swimming pool over at the Alexander H. Stephens State Park. Most of the blacks in the county did not even know that there was a public swimming pool over there even though it was paid for by taxes from both black and white people.

At the mass meeting on a Friday night, we made the decision to go to the park that Saturday morning to integrate the state public swimming pool. All of the black people in the county were not in support of what we were doing, however. They would say things like "It's not our time" or "Don't force integration; just let it happen." Well, my thoughts on that were that we have been waiting for over 400 years and how long should we wait? If not now, when?

I must say that all of the white people in Taliaferro County were not racist people. I remember one of the white merchants, Owen Lunsford, was very nice to us as we were picketing in front of his store. It was hot that summer, and Mr. Lunsford would offer us some water or speak to us in a kind voice. I sometimes felt guilty for picketing in front of his store. I really believed he was a real true Christian man.

As we were quietly planning to go over to the park that Saturday morning, the word had gotten back to the white residents of our plan. We were then informed that potash and other chemicals had been put in the swimming pool. It was said, "When those niggers get in that pool, the lye will take the hide off 'em." Despite the warning, we marched over to the park with full intentions of getting into the pool. Everyone had their swimming attire. As we gathered around the pool, everyone was afraid to get in because we did not know for sure whether lye had been put in the pool.

I knew that there were some people in the county who were certainly capable of doing something like that and would have done so because they were angry and filled with hatred, opposing integration at all cost. As we were all standing around the pool, everyone was waiting for someone to get in first to see what would happen.

I heard someone say, "Frank, since you have been leading this far, so lead on now." Knowing that I could not swim, I still jumped into the pool without further hesitation. As I was fighting the water, I dislocated my shoulder. Then everyone else got in once they saw that there was not any potash in the water. Some of the boys who could swim well dove in and got me out the water. Mr. Turner took me to the hospital in Greensboro, Georgia, to have my shoulder put back in place.

I went home after leaving the hospital, but I was told that everyone really enjoyed swimming in that pool. History was made in Crawfordville that day. Those who did not swim got in the shallow part of the pool to get their feet wet. They wanted to be a part of history in Taliaferro County too. All of their lives, they never had an opportunity to swim in that public pool. I do not know whether any of the local white people ever got into that pool again.

That was a milestone for us and all of Georgia because the walls of segregation had started to crumble. I am not saying that the walls have been completely destroyed even to this day. However, since that hot Saturday morning, significant gains and opportunities have been made, but the playing field is still not completely level.

The following Wednesday while resting and recuperating, my shoulder came back out of place. My mother and grandfather took me to the hospital in Washington, Georgia, to put it back in place again. The doctor put my arm in a sling and told me to keep it in the sling for a few days. We did not pay the hospital bill that night, so the next morning, I told Mr. Turner about it. He said he would get SCLC to pay it. I did not hear any more about that bill until approximately three months later.

During that summer, the City of Crawfordville hired a black man by the name of Jessie Meadows as the chief of police. Meadows was given a badge, gun, and new khaki shirt and pants as his police uniform. We all knew the reason he was selected. He was to arrest the protesters so it would not appear that it was whites against blacks. He was hired to do their dirty work. Meadows had very little formal education, and according to an article in the *Atlanta Journal-Constitution,* he had served time in prison for making and selling moonshine. He was given instructions by the powers that be to keep us in line.

Meadows was put on as chief of police on a Thursday, and he instructed us on that same day to clear the streets. We were picketing in a single-file line in front of two stores on the back street, which was commonly referred to as the "colored side." We were not blocking the entrance to the stores, and we were not impeding the flow of pedestrian traffic on the sidewalks. Meadows put his hand on his gun as he shouted to us to "clear the street." I told the students to disperse and clear the street because someone could get hurt or even killed.

The next day, Friday morning, we continued our protest by picketing the stores in a peaceful and orderly manner. Chief Meadows approached me and instructed me to "turn around and clear the street."

I told him, "We aren't in violation of any city ordinance, and we have a right to be here."

"You are under arrest," he replied. He then put the handcuffs on me and marched me up to the courthouse to the sheriff's office. Once there, Chief Meadows asked the sheriff to take the handcuffs off me because he did not know how to unlock them. The sheriff put me in jail and charged me with failing to obey a police officer.

The students still continued their activities. By putting me in jail, it just intensified the activities. In fact, a massive demonstration took place the next day. Sheriff Moore said that if we did not disburse, he would put us all in jail. He did not know that the threat of going to jail did not scare or derail us from our commitment and mission. So many people were protesting and willing to go to jail if necessary. The sheriff would have to let everyone out because the jail could only accommodate approximately 10 or 15 people, and there were approximately 200 or 300 protesters all willing to go to jail.

Chief Meadow's son Jessie Meadows Jr. came down from Atlanta after hearing over the news what was going on. He started protesting with us. He was a nice person and offered to buy the students cold drinks while they were protesting and picketing the stores. He told me that his father was not going to stay on as chief of police. After another massive protest that Saturday evening, we never saw Mr. Meadows again in his police chief uniform. He was the first black chief of police in Georgia and possibly in the South.

The opposition believed that by taking the leaders out of the picture, it would stop the movement, but that did not happen. I had been arrested, and Mr. Turner was jailed several times. That, however, intensified the activities even more. Furthermore, that tactic did not derail our commitment as leaders.

The SCLC had a serious commitment to the Crawfordville movement. Dr. King came to Crawfordville to speak at Friendship Baptist on October 11, 1965, after hearing all of the reports and news accounts of the way the students were being treated. After the rally, we made the decision that it was too dangerous for Dr. King to lead the night march downtown to the courthouse. Instead, Rev. Andrew Young led the march to the courthouse, and Dr. King waited at Lula Stewart's house on Lexington Avenue, which is now Martin Luther King Jr. Drive. There were untold numbers of civil rights workers in Crawfordville during that long hot summer.

The movement was serious, not about fun and games. Many families were evicted from their houses for allowing their children to participate in the movement. Without any warning, a white landowner would come to the houses of black families and say, "Since your child is involved in that civil rights mess, you have to move now."

Some local white men in the county were terrorizing black people at night. They were referred to as the Hubbard Brothers, which consisted of three or four brothers all from Crawfordville. Of course, there were other locals who joined in with them as they intimidated the protesters. I remember a young black man was driving in Crawfordville one night, and a group of white men ran his car off the road, causing his windshield to bust. He reported it to the sheriff, but nothing was done. These types of incidents happened many times without any arrests.

An elderly black man who was not involved in the civil rights movement, George Turner, was stopped one night and beaten. He was mistaken for Mr. Turner's family. George Turner and Calvin Turner were not related, but the Klansmen who came from out of town did not know that. This incident was reported to the sheriff, but just like all of the other reports, nothing was done.

Calvin Craig and the Grand Dragon of the Ku Klux Klan (KKK) came to Crawfordville and held several Klan rallies and cross burnings in an effort to intimidate black folks and get the local whites stirred up. It was my understanding that there were local informants in the ranks of the KKK, and we got information that the Klan was going to kill or do bodily harm to Calvin Turner and me. That entire summer was obviously a very tense and stressful one.

I lived down a dirt road in the Level Hill community out in the country, approximately three miles from the highway. I would never venture down that road at night by myself because we were told that the Klan staked out that dirt road to our house. I had an aunt, Tilly Bates, who lived in the city of Crawfordville, so I used to stay in town with her at night instead of having to travel to our house alone. I knew that the Klan was capable of doing anything, and nothing would be done about it. I also knew to take all necessary precautions because I was well aware of what had happened to those three civil rights workers, Goodman, Chaney and Schwerner, in Philadelphia, Mississippi, a few years earlier. I would constantly tell the students to be careful and to not be caught out alone at night.

The boycotting the stores and protesting continued the entire summer of 1965. Every Sunday, we would meet at the Friendship Baptist Church and then March downtown to the courthouse for a mass rally on the courthouse lawn. We would have prayer, sing freedom songs, invite various speakers to address the protestors, and then march back to the church. Reverend Andrew Young, Hosea Williams, Willie Bolton, Ben Clark, and many others would either pray or address the group as well. Sometimes 200-300 people would be in attendance. Many came from the surrounding counties to participate because they believed in what we were doing, and many of them wanted to get something like that started in their communities.

Representative Tyrone Brooks from neighboring Warren County got involved in the movement as a result of the activities in Crawfordville. Hosea Williams later recommended Brooks to Dr. King to become one of SCLC staffers. After meeting with Dr. King, he hired Tyrone as one of his freedom fighters. Tyrone has been on the battlefield ever since, fighting injustice and for the rights of the little people and the voiceless. Tyrone continued his fight for injustice and discrimination in the state legislature, where he has been serving with distinction for more than 30 years.

Toombs McClendon was instrumental in fighting for the rights of blacks in Washington, Georgia. He was from a prominent, successful family in Washington, Georgia, another neighboring county. He would come over and lead marches downtown to the courthouse on Sundays. He was easily recognizable because he was a huge light-skinned man.

On one particular Sunday, as we were marching downtown to the Courthouse to hold our usual Sunday rally, we noticed a white man with what appeared to be a Bible in his hand. He also had a record player set up on one side of the courthouse lawn playing religious songs. Mr. Turner and I instructed everyone to move over to the right side of the courthouse lawn so we would not interfere with him. There were approximately 200 of us assembled on the lawn, as we had done every Sunday for the last three months.

We held our rally and then we marched backed to the church. There were many hecklers and spectators sitting on cars and standing in the street. The next morning, we learned that warrants were being issued for me, my 70-plus-year-old grandfather, Calvin Turner, and both his father and grandfather. These men had never been arrested for anything in their lives. Like I said, there were approximately 200 participants, but the powers that be selected just four or five participants to charge with disturbing public worship.

The public worship in question was the white man on the courthouse lawn playing religious songs. The reason my grandfather and Calvin Turner's father and grandfather were selected because they thought by arresting and locking up our grandfathers that would cause us to stop our protesting. That tactics did not work. When the word got around the county that these elderly men had been arrested, people who had not been involved in the movement got involved and started participating in mass meetings and donating money and opening their homes to the many civil rights workers that Hosea Williams had ordered to come to Crawfordville for a massive movement. The Crawfordville movement dominated the national and local news for more than two months.

CHAPTER 5

SCOPE

P ending the passage of the Voting Rights Act, Dr. King and SCLC initiated a program called the Summer Community Organization and Political Education (SCOPE) Project for the express purpose of educating blacks about politics and helping them to register to vote. SCOPE took place during the summer of 1965, growing out of SCLC's participation in the Voters Education Project (VEP). SCOPE was also inspired by the Mississippi Freedom Summer Project in 1964, which was launched by the Council of Federated Organizations (COFO). The initiative mobilized hundreds of white college students to work in the South against segregation and black disenfranchisement.

Following the momentum of the Selma to Montgomery march, the SCLC sought to highlight the voter registration process for blacks while the Voting Rights Act was pending in Congress. The SCLC's Voter Registration and Political Education Director, Hosea Williams, was selected to manage the SCOPE effort. On April 30, 1965, Dr. King and now U.S. Congressman John Lewis announced that the two organizations would cooperatively work to implement programs designed to carry out a program of voter education and political mobilization across the South.

Despite promises that the Voting Rights Act would be enacted by June 1965, SCOPE began that summer as the bill winded its way through Congress. More than 1,200 SCOPE workers, including 650 college students from across the nation, 150 SCLC staff members, and 400 local volunteers, served in six southern states to register Blacks to vote.

Prior to the Voting Rights Act, the registrar would require black people to read a passage from the Constitution and interpret what they had read or they would ask questions, such as how many bubbles are there in a bar of soap and many other outlandish requests, all in an effort to deny them the right to vote. With the passage of the Voting Rights Act, all that was required for a person to register to vote was to sign their name. This was a very radical change for black folks.

Dr. King and the staff of SCLC had recruited students from college campuses from around the country to come to the South to help educate black people about the Voting Rights Act and encourage them to go out and register to vote. These students were courageous and committed. They knew of the danger that existed in the rural South for white people working with and helping black people. In spite of the looming danger, they still came to help. The students were paid $15 per week, and they lived in the homes of black families.

There were several civil rights workers in Crawfordville during the "long, hot summer of 1965," and Hosea Williams sent four SCOPE workers – all were White – on June 15, 1965. There were two young women and two men. Canda Webber was an 18-year-old college student from Seattle, Washington. Judy Van Allen was 24 years old from California; she had just graduated from UCLA Berkeley graduate program. Richard "Dick" Copeland was a 19-year-old college student from Oregon. Father Joseph Cooney was a Catholic priest from Washington, DC. Father Cooney had just graduated from law school and taken the bar exam, and he was awaiting his results while working with the SCOPE Project in Crawfordville.

Father Cooney was one of the bravest and most inspiring people I had ever met. I remembered one of our many conversations when he asked me one day about my future plans. He asked, "How can you help your people by cutting pulp wood and chopping cotton?" Those words remained with me for the next 45 years.

Before that conversation with Father Cooney, I had never thought about going to college. I did not even know whether I was college material. I was like most of the boys in Crawfordville. I just wanted to finish high school, go to Atlanta, get a job, and buy a car. I could not see a future for me other that doing what many others from Crawfordville had done.

Dr. Evan Harris, our high school principal, had encouraged me to stay in high school because I had decided to quit after my father had died in February 1964. I decided to go to Athens, Georgia, and get a job in the chicken poultry plant. Meanwhile, I could help my mother with the farm. After applying for the job, they were showing me around the plant, explaining the job. As I was walking through the plant, I got sick on the stomach from the fresh smell of chicken. I knew then that I could not work there. I even developed a distaste for chicken from that point. In fact, I do not eat chicken today because of that poultry plant visit. Dr. Harris suggested that I consider going to Job Core instead of dropping out of school. With my mother's encouragement, however, I decided to stay in school.

Father Cooney told me that I needed to go to college, and he said that if I would go to a prep school for two years, he would get me a scholarship to George Washington University in DC. I promised Father Cooney that I would go to a prep school and take him up on his offer. Beyond just me, these four SCOPE workers gave hope to many black people – both young and old. They inspired the young and gave hope to the adults that their children will have a better life than they had.

On July 23, 1965, Dick, the college student from Oregon, was beaten on the courthouse square by two white men and told to leave town. Still, these SCOPE workers were able to register 100 black people to vote and taught them the importance of voting. Almost every eligible voter in the county was registered as a result of their efforts. Today, the voters of Taliaferro County have been able to elect several African Americans to city and county positions. Now the majority of the City Council members are black and a majority of the county commissioners are black.

President Lyndon B. Johnson signed the Voting Rights Act on August 6, 1965. SCOPE ended three weeks after its enactment, depriving the SCLC workers, students and local volunteers of federal support during most of the program. Dr. King reported that most of the project goals had been achieved, and he projected success in SCLC's future registration efforts. The long, hot summer of 1965 ended in September. The civil rights workers left for other hot spots around the country, and the SCOPE project ended. The SCOPE workers went back to their homes with a wealth of knowledge and experiences. They said that they would "never forget" their summer in Crawfordville. Overall, the SCOPE project was successful throughout the South.

During that summer, parents and students made the decision not to go back to Murden in the fall, so they contacted the superintendent to register to attend the white school, Alexander H. Stephens. The 83 black students who applied there continued their efforts to integrate the school system in the county. To our surprise and without our knowledge, the superintendent and the school board had secretly conspired to bus all of the white children to the surrounding counties, including Wilkes, Greene, Warren and Oglethorpe Counties in order to avoid integration of the school.

Evidence revealed that the superintendent assisted the white teachers in finding jobs in some of the surrounding counties as well. We learned of this clandestine effort the night before the white children were to be bused to the surrounding counties on buses paid for by state and local taxes. Once we learned of what was going to take place, we mobilized our students that night and instructed them to meet at the Alexander H. Stephens gym, which was the point where the white children would meet and board the buses that would take them to the surrounding counties for school.

We came early that morning prepared to board the buses along with the white children. We said if white children can ride the tax-supported buses to the surrounding counties, then we should be able to enjoy that same privilege. As we made our attempt to board the buses, the local sheriff and state troopers blocked our effort. I instructed the students to lie down in front of the buses in an effort to prevent the buses from carrying the white students without taking us. Those brave and committed students lay down on the ground in front of those buses. Both boys and girls knew that they could get run over just one or two feet from those big tires. The streets were wet, but the students lay down on the wet pavement anyway. The bus driver refused to proceed, so a local white man said, "Let me get on and drive the bus. I will run over those niggers."

He got on the bus and raised the engine real loudly several times, but we did not flinch. We were scared, but we could not let him know that. The state trooper immediately jumped on the bus, shut off the engine, and took the man off of the bus. Eventually, the state troopers dragged us away and allowed the buses to proceed. We continued this attempt for several mornings with the same result. One particular morning, we formed a car pool and followed the buses to Warrenton, Georgia. We said that if they wouldn't let us ride the buses, then we would drive our own cars to the school.

I was driving a 1951 Chevrolet that my brother had bought me, and as I approached the school in Warrenton, a sea of hecklers from Crawfordville and a wall of state troopers were aligned in front of the school. As I got closer to the school, my car got hit with an egg. I was attacked, pulled out of the car and beaten until the troopers pulled the mob of white men off me. The troopers were instructed to keep the violence down because they did not want another scene like what had taken place about a year ago at the Edmund Pettus Bridge in Selma, Alabama. We were prevented from entering the school, and the state troopers escorted us out the county back to Crawfordville.

CHAPTER 6

FREEDOM SCHOOL

A fter several attempts were made to enter the school, but to no avail, we decided to concentrate our efforts on attending a Freedom School in the Springfield community near Mr. Turner's home. Dr. King and the SCLC had sponsored Freedom Schools throughout the South. We said that we would rather attend a Freedom School instead of going to a segregated school. We refused to attend our old Murden High School, and there were no white children at Alexander H. Stephens. The Freedom School was the only viable alternative. Certified teachers were teaching the classes and the students were doing well.

We formed car pools and went throughout the county picking up children, taking them to the school and bringing them back home after classes were finished. The Freedom school operated for several months. One particular morning, we went out picking up children school, and I saw two boys, Otis and Rudolph Mayes, standing beside the road. I asked if they were going to the Freedom School, and they said yes. They got in the car, and we drove to school. Their mother told the sheriff that her sons had gone to the Freedom School without her knowledge. Later that day, the sheriff came to the school and presented me with a warrant, charging me with kidnapping.

Rudolph and Otis were about my age. Their mother did domestic work at some of the white families' houses in Crawfordville. Mrs. Mayes was a good Christian lady, and she had no hatred or ill intent at all toward us. She just didn't know what to do. I talked to them many years later, and they confirmed the fact that I did not kidnap them nor did I take them without their own free will. They wanted to go to the Freedom School because that was where all of the fun was and all of their friends were there too.

The Freedom School was important and exciting because it allowed us a break from our traditional school. It was laid back, relaxing and a fun place to learn. It was not a place just to hang out at all day, however. We all were committed to learning and integrating the public school in Crawfordville.

CHAPTER 7
IN THE COURTS

While these attempts were being made to board the buses, a team of civil rights attorneys were preparing to file a lawsuit in the Federal District Court in Augusta, Georgia. Attorney Howard Moore, Jr., Attorney Donald Hollowell, Attorney Jack Ruffin, and a few others led the team. Each of these lawyers went on to prominence. Howard Moore, Jr. was asked to move to California to be the lead attorney in representing Angela Davis, who was charged with murder and shooting up the courthouse in California in the early '70s. President Lyndon Johnson appointed Donald Lee Hollowell to the Federal Court. Bankhead Highway was changed to Donald Lee Hollowell Boulevard in his honor. Jack Ruffin was appointed to the Georgia State Court of Appeals, where he became the Chief Judge of that court.

On October 22, 1965, the petition was heard by the Federal District Court in the southern district of Georgia, a three-judge panel including Circuit Judge Griffin Bell, and District Judges Frank Scarlett and Lewis Morgan. Calvin Turner was the lead plaintiff in "Turner vs. Goolsby" along with Joseph Turner, James T. Bates, Moses King, Robert Billingsley, Albert King,

Evans Harris, John Wesley Combs, Frank Bates (me), Mary Bates (my mother). This petition was in four counts. Count one contended that a Georgia Code § 26-6901 was unconstitutional. That statute provided that any person charged disturbing religious worship was guilty of a misdemeanor. Mr. Turner had been accused of forging the names of Edna Swain on petitions to enter her children in Alexander H. Stephens. Thus, count two contended that the forgery statue, Georgia Code § 26-3914, was unconstitutional, so it sought to restrain its enforcement. Count three contended that the defendants, Kenneth Goolsby, district attorney of the Toombs Judicial Circuit; Sheriff Milton B. Moore; Harold F. Richards, county attorney; Lola Williams, county school superintendent; the local board of education; and others had participated in attempts to deny us, the plaintiffs, of their civil rights. Count four sought the desegregation of the public school system of Taliaferro County.

The defendants filed a counterclaim against us barring us from disturbing classes at Murden High School during school hours and interfering with school buses being used for transporting white students to the schools in surrounding counties. Their claim also contended that the Georgia statutes being challenged were, in fact, lawful and constitutional.

The court decided after hearing testimony from both sides that all 87 students who had registered to attend Alexander H. Stephens (white school) are entitled to attend a desegregated school. The court said that the board of education in Taliaferro County would have to open the white school for both black and white students to attend together or arrange for the black children to attend the same schools and ride the same buses as the white students.

CHAPTER 8
ATTENDING INTEGRATED SCHOOLS

Shortly after the court's decision, the superintendent notified each one of us that we would be attending the same schools that the white students were attending. I was selected to attend the Wilkes County School along with five other girls. It was no accident that only one boy was sent to a school along with five girls.

There were 87 students to be divided between three schools. There was relatively an equal amount of boys and girls. No consideration was given to how close you lived to a particular school because there were students closest to Warrenton, but they were assigned to Greene County. There were students closest to Washington, but they were assigned to Warrenton.

I felt that the reason I was assigned to Washington as the only boy was because they felt that if for some reason they could stop me from going to school, then the others would stop and go back to Murden. It did not turn out the way they had planned, however. Fred Luneford was driving the bus that took the students to Wilkes County. He came to our house one evening and told my mother and me that he would be picking me up the next day and the time he would be at my house.

The next day was a historic day in Taliaferro County and

possibly throughout rural Georgia. Before that day, no black student had ever ridden on the same bus with white students. When the bus came that morning, I was standing out in front of our house along with my mother by my side, as she had done throughout the movement. When I got on the bus, all of the white children had already been picked up and were seated. I was the only black student on the bus. The white students were not mean to me on the bus; they just did not say anything to me. I am quite sure they were briefed and told not to say or do anything to me.

As our bus approached the school in Washington, I saw a lot of white spectators outside. I can assure you that they were not a part of any welcoming committee. The word had gotten around that we were enrolling in the white school that morning, and they wanted to be on hand to witness this unfortunate, for them, historic event. Before the six of us enrolled in the Wilkes County High School that morning, there had never been a black student in that school. When I got off the bus, I was met by one of the school's administrators and directed to the principal's office, where I met the other five girls. The principal, Mr. Anderson, talked to us about our homeroom and class assignments, and he suggested that we not use the student restroom but instead use the faculty restroom. I am quite sure he did not want any problems at his school, and he had a briefing session with the faculty and students the day before.

I found my homeroom and took my seat in one of the chairs. I felt isolated because none of the students wanted to sit near me. That was no surprise to me because they were experiencing something that they had never seen before. This was new to me also. When we changed classes and I was walking down the halls, the students made sure that they did not bump into me or get close to me. The first day went off without a hitch and no problems other than the looks I would get from the students.

The next day the bus picked me up at the same time. As we were heading into Washington, Sheriff Cecil Moore stopped the bus and asked the driver, Mr. Luneford, "Do you have a Frank Bates on this bus?"

He replied, "Yes, sir, I do."

The sheriff then ordered me off the bus, saying, "I have a warrant for your arrest." He shoved me in the backseat of his car. I asked the sheriff why I was being arrested, but he said nothing. Instead, he threw the warrant in the back seat where I was sitting. I read the warrant as he drove away, and it indicated that I was charged with writing a bad check. I was 17 years old, and I had never written a real check in my life other than in school when the teacher would teach us about finance and how to fill in the appropriate blanks on the face of a check.

The sheriff took me to the courthouse and put me in jail. He allowed me to get in touch with my mother and grandfather to let them know what happened. My grandfather asked to go on my bond, but the Sheriff told him that he would only accept a Wilkes County property bond. My mother contacted Mr. Turner and made him aware of what happened. Mr. Turner tried desperately to get someone from Wilkes County to go on my bond. Finally, late that night, he got in touch with a businessman in Wilkes County by the name of Marion Harden. Most people knew him as "Snook Harden." Snook was in the pool table and jukebox business. He supplied almost all of the pool tables and jukeboxes to the black cafes and juke joints in the surrounding counties.

The Sheriff had discouraged people from going on my bond by telling them that they do not need to get involved in that civil rights mess. He tried to discourage Snook by telling him that the white folks in Wilkes County thought a lot of him, and they would not like it if he went on my bond. Snook told the Sheriff that he did not make one dime off white folks and that all of his pool tables and jukeboxes were in black folks' businesses. He signed my bond that night. The Sheriff could not intimidate Snook because he was known by many standards, at that time, as being independently wealthy. For a long time, I did not know he was black because he looked very much like white people. I got out of jail late that night, and went home to get ready for school the next day.

The warrant alleged that I wrote and gave Dr. Wills a bad check. Dr. Wills was the doctor who put my shoulder back in place when my mother took me to the emergency room for a dislocated shoulder. He later sent my mother a bill for $75. Mr. Turner told my mother to give him the bill and that he would send it to Dr. King for them to pay for my hospital service. Calvin sent the bill to the SCLC and they sent Dr. Wills a check for the full amount. That was the last time I heard about a check, and I never even saw the check that SCLC sent to Dr. Wills. Either Dr. Wills or the hospital administration held the check for some unknown reason. All I know is that the issue of a bad check did not surface until I enrolled in school in Wilkes County.

The third day of school began the same way. The bus driver picked me up at the same time, and again, no one said anything to me. They were neither mean to me nor was I mean to them. My bus made the trip to the school without being interrupted like the day before. I went to my homeroom class to begin the school day. The next period, we changed classes, and I reported to the shop class, which was the building away from the main building. During class, I noticed that the students were talking and laughing among themselves. I did not know what was going on. When the bell rang, I noticed that all of the children rushed out of the classroom, causing me to be the last person coming out the room. When I walked out, someone hit me about the head, almost knocking me down, but I was able to maintain my balance. I ran to the principal's office and told Mr. Anderson what had happened. He neither offered me any sympathy nor was I looking for any. I knew going in that it was not going to be an easy transition.

The principal told me to just "stay out of their way for the rest of the day."

I asked, "How can I stay out of the way of 500 students?"

He said, "Do the best you can."

I told my teacher Mr. Andrews that the left side of my face was really hurting, and he told me to go the teacher's lounge and lie down. My face started swelling to the point that I could not open my mouth. I did not eat lunch because of the swelling. I expected things like this because I had seen footage of what the black students in Little Rock, Arkansas, had gone through back in 1957 when they integrated Central High School. I also saw what Charlene Hunter and Hamilton Holmes went through in 1962 at the University of Georgia.

I was not seeking any notoriety or playing for the media because all of the media people had gone. This journey was never about getting on TV, seeing myself on the six o'clock news or reading about me in the newspapers. This was all about racial equality and not being treated as second-class citizens. I knew that we were just as smart and intelligent as anyone else. Equal opportunity is what we were seeking – no more and no less.

At the end of the school day and before I left to go home, the principal gave me a letter which indicated that I had been suspended from school because it was against the school's policy for any student to attend that school if they had been in jail and still under a bond.

Yes, I was still under a bond for the trumped up charge of writing a bad check. I started thinking about why Dr. Wills or the hospital authorities held that check all those months. I did not want to believe that this was all calculated. I did not have much faith in that so-called school policy because one of my classmates who was accused of murder was still in school, and he was not suspended. He was charged with the beating death of a black boy at the bus station in Washington the year before. While I do not have any knowledge as to whether or not he was out on bond at the time, I do know that he was eventually acquitted. It appeared to me that a charge of murder is more serious than a charge of writing a bad check.

I showed the letter to my mother and told her what had happened. By then, my jaw was swollen and my ear was hurting, so my mother and grandfather took me to the doctor in Union Point, Georgia that evening. The doctor examined my jaw and determined that it was not broken but severely bruised. On my way home from the doctor's office, I could tell that my grand-father was becoming a little impatient about my involvement in the civil rights movement. He, admittedly, had endured a lot because of me. He was in his late 80s, and I seriously doubt that he would have been involved in the civil rights movement to the extent that he was if it had not been for me.

I was in my senior year of high school, and in a few short months, I am supposed to be graduating. I was faced with the serious dilemma of being retained in the 12th grade or consider going back to my old high school (Murden). I made the decision to go back to my old high school a few days later. The principal said that he would have to check with the superintendent to see if I could come back to Murden. The superintendent immediately notified the principal and told him, "Frank Bates has tried to go to school everywhere else, and we don't want him back at Murden anymore."

My brother Fred came home for the Thanksgiving holiday, and my grandfather told him to take me back to Atlanta because he said, "Enough is enough." He wanted me out of the county because he feared for my life.

I went to Atlanta to live with my brother the Monday after Thanksgiving in 1965. Immediately, I started looking for a job. I was able to find my first job at the Piedmont Driving Club near Piedmont Park as a dishwasher for $1 per hour. I worked there for approximately two weeks, and then they told me that I would have to work during the Christmas holiday and Christmas day. I decided to quit because I had never been away from my home in Crawfordville on Christmas. Furthermore, my mother's birthday is on the 25th day of December, and I wanted to be with her on Christmas morning.

Finding another job in those days was not a big deal because jobs were easy to find back then. My next job was at Simmons Plating Works on Whitehall Street. Several of my friends from Crawfordville worked there and they aided me in getting a position. I worked around the clock (24 hours) one day. I was trying to earn enough money to make a down payment on a car. Like I said, I did not have any ambition after high school. I wanted to do what most of the boys from Crawfordville had done before me, which was move to Atlanta, get a job, and then get a car.

Well, I was able to earn enough money to make a down payment, but I needed a co-signer, someone who had good credit. I asked my brother Gordon, and he agreed to co-sign for me. I bought a 1958 Pontiac. I cannot remember the amount that I paid for the car, but my payments were $50.00 per month for 12 months. I probably paid the total value of the car in my initial down payment, but that car served me well.

While working at Simmons, someone told me about evening school at Booker T. Washington. Booker T. Washington was one of two schools in Atlanta for blacks. David T. Howard was in the 4th Ward, and Booker T. Washington was on the West Side on Hunter Street. Back then, Booker T. Washington was considered the place where "big shots" attended.

I started checking into the school and seeing what I needed to do in order to enroll. I definitely wanted to finish high school since I was suspended in Wilkes County and banned from my hometown school in Crawfordville. The school administrators explained to me exactly what I needed to do in order to enroll, and they told me the purpose of evening school. The school was designed for people who wanted to complete their high school education because they had to work during the day and for girls who were put out of the regular day school because they had gotten pregnant. During those days, girls could not go to the regular day school if they were pregnant.

The school fit my needs, and I told my two other friends and former classmates Eddie Andrews and Johnny Cleveland Peek about it. We had been in the same class room since the 2nd grade. They too were involved in the civil rights movement and were out of Murden high school.

The evening school fit my needs. It allowed me to go to school at night while I worked during the day. Once I got a copy of my transcript and mailed it to Booker T. Washington, I started taking classes in January of 1966. I was able to graduate in May of that same year. I was so happy because I was able to graduate from high school in spite of the obstacles I had encountered.

CHAPTER 9

STARTING COLLEGE

While working for Avon Cosmetics Company, one of the many jobs I had, I met someone there who told me about Dekalb Junior College. I then started checking into the requirements for enrollment. I remembered what Father Cooney had told me the summer while he was in Crawfordville working with the civil rights movement. He said if I were to complete a two-year college, then he would help me to get a scholarship to George Washington University in DC. I got in touch with Father Cooney and told him that I had finished high school and was about to enroll in a junior college. He asked me to keep in touch with him and let him know when I finished my two years at DeKalb Junior College.

I was able to complete all of the requirements for enrollment in the college, so I began attending in January 1967. This was a completely different experience for me. Even though, I had gone to school with white children in high school in Wilkes County for only two days, this formal integration seemed foreign to me. Dekalb Junior College was predominantly white then. There were approximately 10 men and three women enrolled in the college when I started in January.

All of the students there were nice, nothing like what I had experienced earlier in high school in Wilkes County. At the end of my first quarter, I had a 0.66 grade point average. I had two Fs and a D. I did not even have a full grade point average. It was not because I was slow; it was because I did not know how to study. I remembered my mother telling me that I could stay at home and make an F. The school sent me a notice indicating that I was placed on academic probation for a quarter, and if I failed to get off of probation the next quarter, then I would be asked to leave the college. I know I had disappointed a lot of people, including myself. Many of my family members had sacrificed greatly for me. I was staying with my brother Fred and his wife, Sadie, and they were not charging me any money for living with them. I am eternally grateful and deeply indebted to them for taking care of me while I was in school. I decided that if they were doing all of those generous things for me, at least I could help myself by studying and passing my courses.

Not only did Fred let me drive his 1961 Ford at times, he would give me money for gas. Usually he would give me $1 per day. I would use $0.50 for gas. Gas was $0.21 per gallon at a cut-rate service station. I would use the other $0.50 for a sandwich and a coke. All of this made me a more determined and persistent student. I went back for my second quarter with the understanding that I had to get off probation. At the end of the quarter, my grades were good enough for me to be taken off probation. After that, I never looked back and I was never placed on academic probation again throughout my college and law school career. My first year ended, as far as I was concerned, on a positive note because I had gotten off probation and through the first year without failing any more classes.

CHAPTER 10

WORKING FOR RANDOLPH T. BLACKWWELL

The year of 1968 was both exciting and sad for me. Dr. King had always surrounded himself with good people who had the interest of poor, common people at heart. One of those people was Randolph Blackwell. Randy, as he was called, was a smart person. He had two master degrees and a law degree from Howard University. He could have practiced law and probably made a lot of money, but he elected to work for the poor and the underserved. He left the SCLC and organized the Southern Rural Action Project. This project was designed to bring economic recovery to rural communities throughout the South. Blackwell came to Crawfordville and headed up a food nutrition program that he had received a grant from the Federal Government to put in place. The program was designed to teach poor people how to prepare food in the most nutritious way.

In 1964, Congress passed the Food Stamps Act, and by 1967, this program was still very new. People throughout the South needed information on the most nutritious ways to prepare food and the type of food they needed to purchase with the food stamps. Blackwell hired several local women, including my mother, to help with the food stamp project, which was pivotal to poor people. Food stamps were available to both black and white people. Many white people in the county qualified for the food stamps, but they did not want to be associated with getting food stamps. Dr. Blackwell organized a sewing plant in Crawfordville with a very lucrative contact, London Fog. The sewing plant employed 30 to 40 people at one time. The sewing plant operated for several years before it was moved to Hancock County. My sister, Dorothy, worked at the plant for several years along with my mother. There was also a daycare center that employed several young ladies. This entire project was a part of Crawfordville Enterprises, a business venture that sought to alleviate poverty for blacks in Taliaferro County. A combined initiative of the SCLC and sister organizations, Crawfordville Enterprises became the largest employer in the county.

I worked with Blackwell in the Atlanta office of the Southern Rural Action Project during 1968. We went across the South setting up projects that would provide jobs and opportunities for blacks in the rural South. Blackwell said that the reason blacks left the South and moved to the North was in search of jobs and opportunities. He said, however, "[blacks] would much rather stay in their own communities where their roots are if only they had some jobs that they could do there." For instance, to overcome black flight to the North, the Freedom Quilting Bee was started in rural Alabama. Women could utilize their sewing skills to make quilts, and Blackwell had someone marketing the quilts across the country. This was a great idea because it would bring women together for socializing and networking, and at the same time, they could earn money for their families.

Mrs. Annie B. Moore Ruff,
my first grade teacher

Calvin Turner

Frank and Dorothy, my sister.
4th Sunday in Sept. 1950 at
camp meeting in Sharon, GA

Murden High School, 1964,
in Crawfordville, GA

Back Street
"Colored side" in
Crawfordville

*Ms. Bonner's Café,
a segregated cafe in
Crawfordville*

*County Courthouse
in Crawfordville*

*(Top) Trip to Europe in Aug. 1968
to study the welfare system
(Left) Graduated from the Atlanta
Law School in 1977*

CHAPTER 11

TRAVELING TO EUROPE

I n 1968, during the time I was working with Dr. Blackwell, he was contacted by someone from the Florence G. Heller School of Social Work at Brandeis University in Waltham, Massachusetts. A group of graduate students in the school of social work wanted to know whether foreigners participated in their country's welfare system like Americans. The school petitioned the Ford Foundation and IBM for enough money to sponsor and send 14 nonprofessional social workers to Europe for a month to gather information regarding European participation in their welfare system. Also that year, the International Conference on Social Welfare was being held in Helsinki, Finland

The students wanted to select a diverse group of nonprofessional social workers from all four corners of the country, from different ethnic backgrounds, as well as some who had an active role in civil rights, human rights or welfare rights. Randy called me in his office one day and told me of this project that the students from Brandeis were proposing. He said, "I would like to submit your name for consideration." He explained that others were being considered as well, but he felt that I had a chance because of my previous involvement in the civil rights struggle.

I was excited about just being considered for such a prestigious honor. I prepared my biography, and Randy submitted it for consideration. My fingers were crossed, and I probably prayed every night because I knew that this would be a trip of a lifetime. I probably asked him several times during the submission process if had he heard anything about the trip.

After several months of not hearing anything, I decided that they had probably selected someone else. Much time had passed and I had forgotten about it. One day, seemingly out of the blue, Randy called me into his office and gave me the news that I had been selected. I was ecstatic that I was about to travel almost half way around the world. No words could explain my excitement because, before this, I had barely been out of the state of Georgia. The timing was perfect because the trip would start in the summer while school was out during my second year. The trip was scheduled to end in September just before I was to return to school for the fall quarter.

There was a lot of preparation for the trip. I had to take pictures, apply for a passport, and get a series of immunization shots. I really did not know what to expect or what they expected from us. Later, they sent us a briefing paper letting us know what they were expected to accomplish from this mission. This was not just a month-long vacation, but this was a fact-finding, evidence-gathering mission. Along with gathering pertinent information that the students could use as they were writing their theses, we would be able to enjoy some historic sites as we traveled across Europe.

The time finally came for me to leave Atlanta for New York. My brother Fred took me to the airport, which was my first trip on a plane. I was afraid or maybe I was more scared of the unknown than afraid of flying. My brother walked with me through the airport and to my plane. Back then, visitors could accompany passengers all the way to the plane to see them board the flight. The plane left on time, and once we were airborne, all of my fears of flying seemed to vanish. The plane landed at Kennedy Airport and I had to find my way to Grand Central Station in downtown Manhattan. This certainly was a long way from Crawfordville, which was apparent in everything I saw, including streets filled with people rushing about and tall buildings flanked with signs.

I took a cab from the airport to the bus station. I do not remember how much the cab fare was, but I can imagine that I probably paid more than I should have. I made it to the bus station and I had about two hours before my bus was scheduled to leave for Brattleboro, Vermont. I decided that I would walk around the streets and really look at New York for the first time. It was "country come to town" for me. I did not want to appear that I was a country boy looking up at all of those tall buildings, but I could not refrain from gawking.

I had been warned by my brothers and those who had been to New York, not to speak to anyone when you pass them on the streets because New Yorkers do not speak to strangers like Southerners do. You can bet that I did not get too far away from the bus station because I did not want to be late and miss my bus. I met a person at the bus station who looked friendly, and he spoke with me since we both were going to Brattleboro. I soon discovered that he was one of the participants, and from that point, we struck up a close friendship. His name was John Troveno from Austin, Texas, a Mexican American. He and his people had been discriminated against just like black people in the South. John said they were referred to as "wet backs," a derogatory name given to Mexicans living in the United States. John was involved in a community action program working with Hispanic children to help alleviate their language barrier and seek job opportunities for their families. We sat on the same seat on the bus, and we probably talked all the way to Brattleboro, sharing experiences and relating our social struggles. With so much in common, we became close throughout the trip and even after the end of the tour.

CHAPTER 12
ARRIVING IN BRATTLEBORO, VERMONT

rattleboro hugs the shore of New England's largest river, the historic highway to the North country, the Connecticut River. The river flows near present-day downtown, where Fort Dummer was built in 1724. Because the growing populace was subject to frequent Indian raids, the English built a fort on the future site of Brattleboro. It became both a secure position and a trading post for the English settlers. More settlers came to the outpost and cleared 200 acres surrounding Fort Dummer in 1752. The town was chartered the next year in the name of the title owner, William Brattle, Jr., a well-known Boston resident. He was a Harvard graduate, preacher, lawyer, doctor, and legislator. Following his military duties, Brattle died in Nova Scotia in 1776 having never visited the town named for him.

The southern Vermont town was scenic and personable. As I expected, they only had a small black population, and everyone was friendly. A bus from the School of International Living met us at the bus station and took us to the campus, where all the 14 participants met for the first time. The school was founded in the midst of the Great Depression. Dr. Donald B. Watt, a former personnel director for Syracuse University, wanted to improve American students' cultural understanding and awareness by having them live with students in other countries for a time. He wanted to humanize people in other parts of the world rather than having them thought of as systematic cultural categories who could be effectively studied from afar. Watt established the Experiment in International Living as a project to transform the students' outlook on the world. The first students departed on a ship from New York bound to Germany in June 1932. The 23 students on board became "trailblazers for thousands," including our group, who have followed in their footsteps, learning to embrace cultural differences while gaining a sensitivity for global issues.

After we met and introduced ourselves, we quickly learned that we all had a lot in common even though we came from different parts of the country and from different ethnic backgrounds. I actually learned a lot about this country from the other participants. All of us were involved in the same type of work and working for the same type of people. These were people who were discriminated against or disenfranchised in one way or another. All of us were trying to make a difference in our respective communities.

The organizers of our group did a remarkable job in selecting the participants. The participants were from every part of the country. They were black, white, Hispanic, American Indian and from all types of socio-economic backgrounds. There were two poor white girls from the Mountains of Appalachia, an American Indian from the Navajo Tribe in Arizona, and a Mexican American from Austin, Texas. Others included a Hispanic lady from the lower eastside in Manhattan, a black lady from Watts in Los Angeles, California. There was a white lady with a British background from Cleveland, Ohio, and a Polish lady from Boston Mass. The black men hailed from Chicago's South Side; Cincinnati, Ohio; Washington, DC; and New York's Bedford Stuyvesant Community. I was the only one from the South.

The students from Appalachia were telling us of the deplorable conditions in their mountain region. According to one of the girl's story, I can see why President Kennedy kicked off his war on poverty by visiting the counties of Appalachia, where more than 50 percent of the population were living below the poverty level. We were able to learn from each other about the economic and social conditions of the poor throughout the country. After spending three days together at the School of International Living, we had a relatively clear picture of everyone's struggles.

At the School of International Living, we were also introduced to some of the dos and don'ts in Europe. We were given instructions on how to count and compare the money in the countries that we would be visiting. The graduate students from Brandise were our team leaders, and they made it very clear as to what they were looking for and what they expected to gain from our fact-finding tour. For instance, during our tour of Holland, each one of us was to stay with a family in order to get a realistic feel of life in a Dutch home. We were given the names of the families before we left the campus in Brattleboro.

CHAPTER 13

HEADING TO EUROPE

The day finally came for us to board a bus to New York, where we would board our flight for Europe. We left Brattleboro on a Saturday morning and arrived in New York that afternoon. Our flight was around 7 p.m., and we were scheduled to land in London on Sunday morning. Because the fog was so heavy and we were running low on fuel, our pilot decided to fly to Dublin, Ireland. He wanted to allow the fog to lift and refuel before resuming our trip to London.

Being a history and political science major, I was excited and intrigued with the historic buildings and monuments. I could not wait for us to visit Westminster Abby, Buckingham Palace, Parliament, and other sites that I had only seen pictures of and read about. We started our tour by meeting with a representative from the British Parliament. After a week in Great Britain, we then left for Scandinavia, Demark, Copenhagen, Stockholm, the Netherlands, Amsterdam, and Rotterdam. Finally, we went to Helsinki, Finland, to attend the International Conference on Social Welfare, which is held every four years. We arrived in Helsinki, the capital and largest city, on a Saturday morning by ship, and we walked from the dock a short distance to the university where we would stay.

On the way to the university, we amused the locals by our mere presence. As I stated, our group was diverse and multi-colored. One lady in the group was named Johnnie Tillman from Watts in Los Angeles. She weighed approximately 200 pounds and had jet-black smooth skin. There was an old man on the street selling flowers as we walked by. He did not speak any English, and, of course, we did not speak any Finnish. He gave Johnnie a bouquet of flowers, bowed his head in a friendly gesture, and took his hand and rubbed her face in a gentle way. Then he looked at his hand to see if her black color came off.

It was so spontaneous that we all wished we could have captured that moment on film. Our tour guide thought we would get upset about the street vendor's gesture. She assured us that he meant no harm or malice. We did not take it that way either. Our tour guide explained that Finnish people had never seen black people before – even on television. This was 1968 when Dr. King had just been killed, and America was ush-ering in the black Power Revolution. Still, the Finnish people we encountered knew little to nothing about blacks, much less the civil rights struggle in America. Cars were stopping in the streets, as people stared at us in amazement. Our tour guide thought that their actions would have caused us to perceive the Finnish people negatively.

We talked to several students at the university, and they too said that they had never seen black people before. Despite that, everyone we met was nice and helpful to us. They seemed to sincerely want to know more about us because they had the concept that everyone in America was rich and prosperous. They had no idea that things were the way they were. We all attended the International Conference on Social welfare, but only one member from our group addressed the conference.

The summer of 1968 was a volatile period in America and around the world. The protests of the Vietnam War on college campuses were grabbing the nation's attention along with the "black Power" chants in the inner cities. Meanwhile, the Republican National Convention was being held in Chicago that summer, which caused bloody protest.

Also during that summer, Russia invaded Czechoslovakia, which produced mass confusion and sparked protests throughout the region. On that Monday morning, we were scheduled to go into Leningrad, Russia, which is now Saint Petersburg, but because of all of the unrest and protest, we could not get a boat or plane out of Helsinki into Leningrad. Thus, we cancelled our trip to Russia. The Finnish people were upset with mighty Russia because they thought that they would be the next small county invaded by Russia. Finland is close to Russia, approximately 90 miles across the Baltic Sea. All of the Finnish bars and pubs stopped selling Russian vodka and any other Russian products. The Russian circus opened in London that same week, but mass protests caused organizers to cancel the remaining events before abruptly leaving the country. We did not know what to expect even though we did know we would be somehow affected by the invasion.

On the day we were scheduled to go to Leningrad, we instead spent an extra day in London touring the sites before we returned home. I don't know for sure, but I felt that the U.S. government was monitoring our activities because of the makeup of our group and the things that were going on in 1968.

When we returned home in late September, each one of

us had to prepare a position paper on our experiences and the things that we learned from community organizers in the various countries and how we could apply what we had learned to our own community. In other words, we compared what they were doing to what was being done in our communities. Once we sent our papers to the graduate students at Brandeis, they compiled all of our suggestions and formulated them into one paper, which was then sent to each of us.

The trip ended on a positive but sad note. We were excited about what we had seen and experienced, but we were sad to leave each other. We had developed a close-knit family. We had all agreed that we would meet for a reunion ten years later in New York. The reunion never took place, but I did keep in touch with some of the participants for a few years. Eventually, I lost contact with most everyone except Milton Bluehouse. Somehow we managed to stay in contact with each other. In 1989, I took a trip out West, and I went out to visit with Milton. In April 2011, I drove back out West and spent several days with Milton on the Indian reservation.

My grandfather, J. T. Bates, was so happy and excited about my trip, and he was glad to see me return safely. He said that he had asked the Lord to let him live long enough to see me return home. The Lord answered his prayer because approximately two weeks after I returned home, he passed away quietly in October 1968.

CHAPTER 14

RETURNING TO SCHOOL

I returned to school after one of the most rewarding experiences of a lifetime. However, now it was time to get back to hitting the books and finishing up my second year of college. By March of 1969, I was completing my second year at Dekalb Junior College. I did not get in touch with my mentor Father Joseph Cooney because I had been talking to my former high school classmates and close friends Joann Richardson and George Turner. They were students at Fort Valley State College, which is now Fort Valley State University. They had been telling me about Fort Valley and urging me to consider attending.

In the fall of 1968, my old high school basketball teammate Melvin Johnson, also a student at Fort Valley, invited me to his homecoming football game. I saw everyone laughing and having a good time just like an old fashioned family reunion. I had heard many times from people who had gone to Fort Valley say that it is like a big family, not just while you are a student there, but also long after you have graduated. I had to make a decision about continuing my education because I was entering my last quarter at Dekalb Junior College.

After talking with the counselor at Dekalb, I inquired about Fort Valley. Later, I received a handbook and an application for the college. I completed the application, submitted the necessary accompanying paperwork and paid the application fee. I asked the registrar's office to mail a copy of my transcript to Fort Valley. This was going to be my first option. If I did not get accepted, I would then contact Father Cooney to take him up on his earlier offer to help me get into George Washington University. Approximately one month later, I heard from Fort Valley informing me that I had been accepted for the spring quarter, which started in March 1969.

I had just met my girlfriend, Shirley Davenport, shortly after I returned home from Europe. Leaving town and her was another matter for consideration. However, I was looking at the big picture, which was continuing my education. Now that I had been accepted, I needed to know how much it was going to cost and where I would get the money to go to Fort Valley. While exploring the tuition, cost of books, and room and board, I ran into Jack Young, another old friend from Washington, Georgia. He attended Fort Valley, and his twin sister, Jackie, did also. He told me that the rooming house he was living in had an additional bed for rent. He said he would speak to the landlord to find out if she had rented that bed to someone else and how much she would charge me for rent.

The pieces started falling into place. Jack got back with me and told me that the room was available and the rent was $20 per month. Fort Valley sent me information letting me know the full tuition cost, including activities fees, and room and board. Room and board cost $312 per quarter, and tuition alone was $120. Between my brothers and my mother, I was able to come up with the money needed for tuition and rent with a little left over for food and books.

The day finally came. My brother C. W. Bates drove me to Fort Valley, and he spent the weekend down there with me. Everything was fine until he left to go back to Atlanta that Sunday evening and reality set in with me. This was going to be the first time that I had ever made my home away from family. I initially felt deserted and lonesome; however, that did not last long. The next day, I walked around the campus, and I found my way to the gymnasium, where the registration for classes was held. I met another student in line by the name of Melvin Copeland from Miami, Florida. I did not know it at that time, be he was a good friend of my childhood friend George Turner. Melvin and I became close friends and have remained friends to this very day. George was living on campus, so after I finished registration, I met him. He introduced me to his friends, who he called "the boys."

I had the best of both worlds as it relates to college life. I went from a school which was 99 percent white to a school that was probably 100 percent black at that time. Both were great experiences that I would not trade for anything. I quickly learned that on a historically black college campus there is a unique lingo. Everyone had a nickname that became as common as his or her legal name. These names lingered too, sticking with an individual for a lifetime. If you were from someone's hometown or close by it, you became the "homeboy" or "homegirl," and your roommate became your "rem."

Talking about nicknames, there were two girls who were close friends but looked very different from each other. One of them had a light complexion, and the other one was dark-skinned. They were dubbed as "Brighter Day and "Edge of Night." These girls did not take offense to their pet names, and they would answer to them as well. Certain students had nicknames that were so prominent that no one knew their real names because everyone called them by their nicknames. Nicknames were not just limited to boys; many girls had prominent nicknames as well. My homeboy's crew of friends, or "the boys," ultimately became my friends. We have been together for more than 40 years. Their names and nicknames are the following:

> Harry Hicks ("Hair")
> George Turner ("Mr. Peabody")
> Melvin Copeland ("Magilla")
> Bruce Williams ("Brush")
> Henry Goshey ("Chuck")
> Thomas R. Yearby ("Roe")
> David Hill ("Cookie Man")

And, yes, I had a nickname given to me by my good friend Melvin. My nickname was "Horse Head." It was funny how that name got pinned to me; of course, the boys know how it came about.

When we heard the word "wildcat," we were not always talking about the school's mascot, which is the wild cat. Sometimes the students were referring to the act of living in the dormitory without paying. Students would find a vacant room or find a student who did not have a roommate and arrange to move in with him. Wildcatting was quite popular at one time. I once wildcatted in Harry and Melvin's room by sleeping on an army cart for a quarter because I did not have money for rent.

As an alumna of Fort Valley, I am now a member of the President's Club, which requires each member to commit $1,000 per year. I do not mind because I feel that I am paying the school back for "wild catting." On a serious note, I feel good about my contribution because I feel that the funds are going toward a worthwhile cause.

I majored in history and political science because I felt that this was the path that I needed if I wanted to pursue a law degree. I had said earlier on that I wanted to be a lawyer not because I could be rich and famous like some of the television lawyers. I wanted to become a lawyer so I would know my rights, what I could and could not do for others and myself. I still remembered Father Cooney and the words he said to me about helping my people.

During the summer of 1965 when we were trying to register black people so they could vote, county officials were telling us what we could and could not do. At that time, I did not know whether that was right or not. For reasons like those I wanted to go to law school so I would know what my rights were and know how to help my people in a legal way.

The students in the history and political science programs became close, and we have remained good friends even to this day. I studied with students such as Earl Lockett from Cordele, Georgia, who is a superior court judge in Albany, and a great Baptist preacher. I could see the judgeship then, but not the preacher. I am honored to call him my friend, and I am eternally grateful for his help and support while I was at Fort Valley. It would probably take another book if I tried to mention all the names or students and instructors who had an impact on my life at Fort Valley.

The years that I spent at Fort Valley can never be underestimated, and I would never want to replace them. The relationships I developed during those two years are immeasurable, and our friendships have lasted for a lifetime. Almost everywhere I go, I meet someone who went to Fort Valley, and they eagerly embrace me with that same spirit of love and friendship we all learned "in the Valley."

I do not want to give the impression that we had parties all the time, which is far from the truth. We worked hard, but we found time to enjoy ourselves after our classes. The city of Fort Valley is a relatively small community with the largest employer being the college itself and the Blue Bird Body Company that manufactures school buses. When I was a student at Fort Valley, the community offered very few places for entertainment for students. Still, that did not bother us because we could always found ways to enjoy ourselves. Drinking beer was the biggest thing going on with the students. Drugs were not a big problem on campus at that time because most of the students were from rural communities throughout Georgia where drugs had not been introduced.

Of all the extracurricular activities, the highlight was a beer drinking contest at Mr. Floyd's trailer. Mr. Floyd had a mobile home that he converted into a beer parlor. During the beginning of the quarter when most students had some money, we would go off campus to Mr. Floyd's place to drink beer. We would buy a quart, and Mr. Floyd would record the number on a board. During one particular sitting, Mr. Floyd recorded that we drank 14 quarts of beer. We were the beer drinking champs at Mr. Floyd's place until some members from the Kappa Alpha Psi fraternity came in and drank 15 quarts. Our record stood for a long time, though, before they came and broke it. Mr. Floyd was a smart businessman. He was in the business of selling beer, so he promoted our championship in an effort to sell more beer. It was good for him, but sometimes a headache for us.

The Vietnam War was going on, and many students wanted to make sure that they maintained their grade point average so they could keep their draft deferment. I still remember my draft number quite well, which was 58, a low number. I completed my coursework on March 12, 1971, and when I got home from college that evening, a letter from the draft board instructed me to report for induction on March 24, 1971.

CHAPTER 15

GOING INTO THE MILITARY

Many veterans were returning home and going to Fort Valley to complete their education, taking advantage of the GI Bill that let the military pay for their education. I got a chance to know many of those veterans, and they gave me some very important tips about surviving in the military. They told me that the best way to make it in the military was to do whatever your superiors tell you to do. I did not have any problems with taking orders and not talking back because my father would tell me something one time and I knew better than to question him or talk back.

I was sworn in on March 24th in Atlanta and was driven by bus to Fort Jackson, South Carolina. I arrived at Fort Jackson late that night, and the next morning we woke up to two inches of snow on the ground. We were instructed not to bring any other clothes with us other than what we had on our backs. I had on a short sleeve shirt, and I was cold. I was introduced to the "hurry up and wait" style in the military real early. For instance, they would say to run to the mess hall and wait in line outside for five or ten minutes. After breakfast, we were marched over to the orderly, where we were given our allowance of clothing, shoes and boots.

My first mistake in the military came when one of the old-timers who was issuing boots asked my shoe size, and I told him that I wore size 12. He gave me a size 13. After I saw that he had given me a size 13, I told him that he had made a mistake. He yelled at me and told me not to tell him how to do his job because he had been issuing boots for troops before I was ever born. I found out later, because of all the running and marching that we had to do, I needed that larger size boot. I thought about what that old lifer had said many times. "Lifer" is the term we give a person who has been in the military for a longtime.

After we were settled into our basic training unit, the drill sergeant started looking for someone to be his field leader. Because I was older than many of the troops in my unit and had finished college, I was selected as the senior trainee field leader for the B-3-1 Unit (Company B, 3rd Battalion, 1st Brigade). During the classification period, I thought that I would get a desk type job since I was a college graduate. To my disappointment, I was assigned to an infantry unit, which meant I had to go in combat. With the Vietnam War still going on, I realized that the Army needed more combat-ready troops than desk workers.

Basic training started on April 5, 1971, and as I was going through it, I remembered what one of the veterans had told me before I left Fort Valley. He said do what you are told, follow orders and don't ask why. At the end of the first week of training, I was selected as the "Outstanding Trainee of the Week." When we graduated from basic training on May 28, 1971, I was selected as the "Outstanding Trainee of the Basic Training

Cycle." After graduation, many of my comrades were leaving Fort Jackson, South Carolina, for their specific job training at other posts. Since I was in an infantry unit, I remained at Fort Jackson for another six weeks of infantry training.

I learned a lot from the military, not just how to be a good soldier but about life, respect for authority, discipline, and honor. These principles have followed me to this very day. While I was stationed at Fort Jackson, I applied for a hardship discharge based upon my family's condition and circumstances. The military examined my application and denied my request, but they gave me an opportunity to resubmit with additional information. I was able to get the requested information, and I resubmitted my application along with letters to my United States Senator, Richard Russell, and my United States Congressman, Robert G. Stephens, explaining the hardship that the military put my family in by drafting me into the Army.

I made many friends while I was at Fort Jackson – both black and white. One of those friends talked me into signing up for jump school (paratrooper) after we had finished our infantry training. He told me that the 101st Airborne Division almost got wiped out in Vietnam, and they were not sending any more paratroopers to Vietnam. They had been pulled back to Fort Campbell, Kentucky. He said that he had a brother in Fort Bragg, N. C., who made one jump per month, and he didn't have to go Vietnam. He convinced me that we could do the same. Upon his insistence, I was transferred to Fort Benning in Columbus, Georgia, to start my three weeks of jump school. At the end of training, each person would be awarded their wings in one hand and orders in the other hand. Almost every one of us had orders for the Republic of Vietnam. I jokingly told him,

"I'll never trust another white boy." Of course, I was just kidding with him because I knew he had no control over the orders.

He shipped out to Vietnam the next week, and I never heard from him again. I was placed in a holdover company because my discharge was pending. My company commander told me that if I did not hear about my discharge by the next week, they would have to send me out to Vietnam with the next crew. After a week had almost passed, I was summoned to the company commander's office. I had prepared myself for the worse, but to my surprise, he told me that my discharge had come back approved. I was really happy because I did not want to go to Vietnam.

In order for a veteran to be eligible for military benefits, he or she must have spent at least six months in active duty. My discharge date was two days shy of six months. I knew I wanted to be able to take advantage of the military benefits like going back to college and purchasing a home on the GI Bill. I went back to my commander and asked if I could stay in the Army for two more days. He yelled at me, saying, "We've been trying to get you out of the Army, and now you're asking to stay in longer."

I explained to him that I wanted to be able to take advantage of the military benefits when I got home. He then told me that he would see what he could do by extending my stay in the Army for two more days. The next day, he informed me that my orders had been changed, and my new discharge date was set for September 23, 1971, therefore giving me exactly six months of active duty in the military. On September 23, 1971, at 10 a.m., I was officially separated from active duty with an honorable discharge.

CHAPTER 16

LEAVING THE MILITARY

I immediately called home and told my girlfriend, Shirley, that I had been discharged from the Army. Shirley and her sisters then started planning our wedding date. On October 23, 1971, exactly one month after leaving the Army, I got married. I did not have any money at the time, so I borrowed $100 from a family friend, Golden Stewart. I used $50 to buy a suit to get married in and used the other $50 to pay for two nights at the Royal Coach Motel in Atlanta for our honeymoon. Shirley was working at the Citizen and Southern Bank, so she had enough money to pay for the wedding and the reception, which was held in her apartment. It was a nice, modest reception, just family and some of her closet friends.

I had just started working with Calvin Turner at the Crawfordville Enterprise, and it was a while before I received a check. Money was tight for both of us. I was able to save enough money to buy a 1968 Volkswagen, which was our only form of transportation for a long time. I worked with the Crawfordville Enterprise for approximately six months before moving back to the Atlanta area. We had been looking for a house while living in Crawfordville with my mother, and we found one we liked and could afford in Decatur, Georgia, a suburb of Atlanta. I was able to use my military benefits to secure the loan. The house cost a whopping $21,500, and monthly payments were $147. I felt I had to get two jobs in order to pay that big mortgage payment.

When I was at Fort Valley and went home on weekends, and my sister was on public assistance at that time receiving $90 per month. My sister would give me $10 to go back to school to help me out, but many times, I did not use that money for the right things. I knew my sister needed that money for her and her two daughters, Teresa and Angela. I said that whenever I got out of college and found a job, I would try to repay my sister by helping with her two children. After we bought the house and moved back to Atlanta, I tried to help my sister with the children's Christmas gifts and school clothes. I even took my sister and the children to North Carolina and Washington, D.C., for their first-ever vacation. I tried to expose the kids to the significant government buildings and monuments in Washington, but they were too young to find any of those sites of interest. They had seen Kings Dominion, an amusement park in Doswell, Virginia, on our way up to D.C., and I said that we would stop and spend some time there on our way back home. Apparently, that was the only thing on their minds. I am glad that I was in their lives as they grew up into young ladies and taken on a life and families of their own.

After moving back to Atlanta, I worked at various jobs, including Warren Refrigeration Company. The human resources director at Warren was from Greensboro, Georgia, and he would hire almost everyone who came from Crawfordville and the Greene County area. Being at Warren was almost like being back home because there were so many people working out there from Crawfordville and the surrounding area. Not long after working there, however, I later applied for a job at Avon Cosmetics Company, a place I had worked for back before I started school at DeKalb Junior College. I was rehired at the Avon Cosmetics Company in June 1972 and worked in various capacities before being promoted to supervisor in the closing and dock section. While at Avon, I made the decision to apply for law school to complete my lifelong dream.

I applied to the Atlanta Law School, a night school program designed primarily for people who worked full time during the day. That school suited my needs because I had a full-time job, and I could not afford to quit my job at the time and go to school. I had to be honest with myself, for I did not know whether I was law school material or not. I decided that I would give it my all, and if during the very first quarter I had failing grades, I would quit.

I started classes in March 1974, going three nights per week, four hours per night from 6 to 10 p.m. I had been out of school for about three years, and I had to make some adjustments to overcome hurdles that would affect my success. I knew it would not be easy, though. Law school was difficult enough, but having to work full time and go to school at night would require an even greater commitment. I burned quite a bit of midnight oil during my first quarter, but with the help of my black law dictionary, I was able to finish and pass all of my courses. Throughout high school, college and law school, I had been just an average student, but I have always been a hard-working, persistent student.

During my third year, I failed corporate law, which was the first course I had failed. I remembered what I said in the beginning about quitting the first time I had failing grades. I had a decision to make: should I hold true to my earlier decision three years prior or retake the course?

I talked to my good friend Randolph Blackwell and my family about my dilemma. Both Randolph and my family said the situation was a no-brainer. Of course, they all said, I should go back and take the course over because I was too close to quit. I, too, did not want to be a quitter, but I was still insecure and second-guessing my adequacy. I went back and took the course from another professor because that instructor was no longer there. I learned later that he was let go because too many students had failed his course. I did not use that as an excuse for me failing the course, though. I placed the blame squarely on me and no one else. No matter how many other students had failed, I was there for me and responsible only for myself. I passed the course with a good grade the second time.

After meeting with the school's administration, they informed me that I had been cleared for graduation in March 1977. After learning of my graduation date, I contacted my old friend Father Joseph Cooney in Washington, D.C., to invite him to my graduation. Father Cooney had just undergone back surgery, so he could not travel. I really wanted him there to observe my graduation because if it had not been for him, I probably would not have gone to college.

As I was preparing for graduation, I knew that I wanted to work in the legal community and I needed a job. One of my friends at Avon made it very clear to me that I needed to leave Avon before I got trapped. He said, "You are working alongside me, and I only have a 6th grade education. You need to go and utilize your legal training."

CHAPTER 17

CONTACTING KENNETH GOOLSBY

I thought about my old adversary, Kenneth Goolsby, who was still the district attorney in the Toombs Judicial Circuit. I called Mr. Goolsby and told him that I was graduating from law school in March and that I needed his help to find me a job in the legal community. He and I talked for a while before he asked me to come and see him. I could not afford to quit my job at Avon until I knew that I had another job. Having a law degree was one thing, but I still needed to earn money.

I have had many highlights and milestones in my life, but I think the greatest feat came on March 16, 1977, the day I marched across the stage at the Atlanta Civic Center and received my Juris Doctorate Degree with my family in the audience. To my surprise, my family members from Cincinnati came to share in my graduation ceremony and celebrate that momentous day. My family has always been very supportive of me. As matter of fact, all of my brothers and sister are close to each other. Our mother would tell us all the time to "stick with each other" and never roll on or take advantage of each other.

"The boys," my old college classmates, came up to celebrate with me at a cookout that Shirley had planned for me after graduation. They were my extended family, as we have been close ever since my first day at Fort Valley back in 1969. All of my family and well-wishers were very proud for me and my accomplishments. After the parties and hoopla, it was time for me to go to work and get on with my life as a lawyer in the legal community. I called Mr. Goolsby's secretary and arranged a meeting with him.

I went down to Thomson, Georgia, to the district attorney's office to meet with Mr. Goolsby. He and I had a good meeting reminiscing and catching up on what I had been doing for the last 12 years since we left court. He said that he was ready to "bury the hatchet" if I was. I told him that I still stood for the same principles I had in 1965, but instead of me marching and lying down in the streets protesting, I knew how to use the legal system to achieve what I used to protest for back then.

He said that he had a position as a special investigator in the child support unit coming available in about a month. This was a federally-funded position designed to locate absent parents who were not supporting their children and were on public assistance. The position was to last for three months working and interfacing with the Department of Family and Children Services (DFACS) in each of the six counties in the Toombs Judicial Circuit.

Dennis Sanders, the assistant district attorney, and I became good friends. Dennis was extremely supportive, and he helped me to fit into my new job with my new work family at the DA's office. I am deeply indebted to Dennis for his friendship and support. Vivian Shoemaker was the secretary in the child support unit, and Robert Ladson was the director. We were a small unit that got along well.

My position at the district attorney's office was a major transition for me because just a few short years prior, I was on the other side of the establishment, defending those being prosecuted and persecuted unfairly. My friends use to ask me how I felt being a civil rights activist and now working with "the man." I would tell them, "I am still Frank Bates, the civil rights activist and supporter of black folks' rights, but I just happen to have a different type of job now."

When I first started with the district attorney's office, there were probably only two other blacks in the DA's offices around the state. I only knew of a black male who was an assistant DA in Atlanta, and a black woman, Evita Paschal, an assistant DA in Augusta. Mr. Goolsby took a lot of heat from some of the white constituents in Crawfordville, Washington and Warrenton for hiring me knowing that I had been active in the civil rights movement in 1965.

I knew there were many just waiting for me to mess up so they could tell Mr. Goolsby, "I told you so." I was also looked at with much skepticism from black folks who were uncertain about my role. When I use to go to social gatherings and parties, sometimes people there would be smoking marijuana. However, when I came in the room, they would put out their cigarettes or dispose of their illegal substance. Someone came up to me one night and said that I was putting a damper on their fun by being there because people at the function was unsure about me and my role. I understood because they had never seen a black person working with the prosecution.

I made some lifelong friends – both black and white – while I was with the DA's office. I remember going to a DA's seminar in Jekyll Island for the first time. My presence was very new to them because they were not use to seeing a black person amongst their ranks. Still, they were all pleasant and accommodating. They all knew me because I stood out like a sore thumb. I established a relationship with many of the DAs and their assistants, which has lasted for more than 30 years.

It is amazing how someone can such an adversary at one time and later those same individuals become friends with mutual respect for each other. I knew Mr. Goolsby did not approve or like what I was involved in back in 1965, but I feel that he respected me for what I stood for back then. He told me many times that he felt that I showed much respect and courage by calling him and asking for help.

At the end of that federally-funded program in three months, the local Department of Family and Children Services directors in the six counties contacted Mr. Goolsby and asked him to find a way to keep me on the job. They said that they felt that I was really helping them to identify and locate some of the absent parents, something that they had not been able to do with much success. Mr. Goolsby went to the county commissioners in each county and encouraged them to put up enough money to continue to support my salary. Just as I was getting settled into my job at the DA's office, Shirley and I made the decision to dissolve our marriage. In October of 1978, our divorce became final after six years of marriage. We did not have any children of our own, but we had the pleasure of helping to raise her cousin's daughter, Shawanda Latrice Hurt, who we called "Tresie." Shirley and I were honored to be her godparents. That relationship still exists to this day, and now I even have a god grandson named Bradrick Hurt. He and his mother live in Greensboro, Georgia.

CHAPTER 18

MEETING JOE FRANK HARRIS

I n 1981, an underdog by the name of Representative Joe Frank Harris from Cartersville, Georgia, was making noise about running for governor of Georgia. I had never heard of Joe Frank Harris, but another good friend from Thomson, named Bobby Harris who was the McDuffie County Tax Commissioner, knew Joe Frank very well and believed that he would make a good governor. Bobby talked to me about Joe Frank and what he stood for on many occasions.

One day, Bobby arranged for me to go to Atlanta to meet Joe Frank. However, before I met with him, I called a good friend of mine named Randy Humphrey from Valdosta, Georgia, who was working for Governor Carl Sanders. I asked Randy about Joe Frank and what kind of person he was. Randy said that he was a respectable Christian person, but he was a dark horse in the race. Randy said that he felt that Congressman Bo Ginn would get the Democratic nomination. I went to Atlanta and met Joe Frank and his assistance, Wayne Reese, who was in his senior year of law school at the University of Georgia (UGA). We had a great meeting and I confessed to Joe Frank that I did not know very much about him. Still, I was willing to support him because Bobby Harris recommended him very highly.

In October of 1981 while attending a homecoming football game at Fort Valley State University, I was almost thrown out of the stadium by my friends for passing out campaign material for Joe Frank. Many of my friends at Fort Valley were educators, and they felt that Bo Ginn supported the views of educators more so than Joe Frank. I do not know how many I convinced that day, but I know as time went on, many of them indicated that they were going to support Joe. Mr. Goolsby was also supporting Bo Ginn because his friend Glen Thomas, the district attorney from Brunswick, Georgia, was a college classmate of Bo and a personal friend.

Joe Frank knew that the black vote would be crucial in the election, so he wanted to make sure that those that needed rides to the polls would be offered a ride. I was assigned to cover all of the counties in my judicial circuit and the surrounding counties. The election was competitive because Congressman Bo Ginn had the ability to raise large amounts of money. During those days, we were not worried about Republicans because they were not a threat in a statewide election. If we were able to win the primary election, then we felt that we were home free in the general election. Surprisingly, Joe Frank won because some of the supporters from the other candidates came over to support him in the runoff. The general election was not as competitive as the primary and the runoff, and as expected, he won the election to become the 78th governor of Georgia.

In February 1983, Governor Harris' senior staff member, Mike De Vegter, called to offer me a position with the Office of Fair Employment Practices. I would be representing state employees who felt they had been discriminated against because of their age, sex, religion, national origin and color.

CHAPTER 19
LEAVING THE DA'S OFFICE

I n March 1983, I resigned my position with the district attorney's office and moved back to Atlanta to start work with the Harris administration, handling employment and discrimination complaints. I served in that capacity for two years after traveling all over Georgia hearing complaints from state employees and individuals who had applied for state positions. That position gave me an opportunity to assist and help those who had been discriminated against in the work place, which was dear cause to me. This, in fact, was the first time that I felt I was making an impact since that long hot summer of 1965.

Governor Harris made some new appointments to the Democratic Party of Georgia in 1985. He appointed his long-time friend John Henry Anderson from Hawkinsville as the chairman of the party, Bobby Kahn as the director, and me as the deputy director. As deputy director, I was responsible for raising money for the party and helping Democrats in local, state and national elections get elected to public office. This job required me to travel the entire state working with the local party chairpersons in an effort to build a stronger state party.

We were ultimately able to organize a local party assembly in each county statewide. As a result of our efforts, we were also able to elect and reelect a countless number of Democrats to public office throughout Georgia. In 1986, Atlanta made the bid to host the 1988 Democratic National Convention along with several other cities. Houston, Texas was our main competition that year, but they had some labor problems, which caused the committee to turn away from Houston. We had some concerns as well, but our problems weren't so major that we couldn't fix them. The DNC committee was concerned about the size of our proposed venue (The Omni) and if it had sufficient floor space to seat the delegates. After several meetings with the construction and engineering teams, we were able to work out the seating arrangements to the satisfaction of the committee.

To my knowledge, this would be the first time that the Democratic Party had held its convention in the South. This was a new for us and a great opportunity for Atlanta and Georgia to be in the national spot light. We had a lot of work to do in order to get ready for the big, weeklong event, in which the eyes of the nation would be on us. One of my many tasks was to travel to every congressional district and hold workshops on the delegate selection process. Many people thought that since the convention was being held in Atlanta that we would get a larger number of delegates and alternates. The number of congressional districts and population would always determine the number of delegates that we would get.

The convention went off without any major disruptions or incidents. Overall, it was a successful, unforgettable event. I was really glad when it was over, however, because I had put in some long hours preparing for it and working during the convention.

While working on my convention duties, I applied for and was certified as a Risk Reduction Instructor, and later opened two DUI schools, initially in Thomson and Crawford-ville. Approximately one year later, I opened one in Decatur and Greensboro, Georgia. I was on the road traveling for the Democratic Party and I needed someone to help me to run the schools, so I asked my longtime friend, Wilhelmena Turman to help me with the classes on weekends. She became certified as an instructor after a series of classes and training that was one of the best decisions I made.

My job became so demanding that Wilhelmena became the primary instructor and administrator of the East Central DUI School. Approximately two years later, my niece Teresa Ken-drick became certified, and she started working with the DUI School as an instructor. Between Wilhelmena and Teresa, they took complete control of the school and ran it like it was theirs. Many times, I did not know how many students we had or how much money we had made. I did not need to know because I trusted them completely.

In December 1985, while attending a Christmas party in Sparta, Georgia, I was introduced to a lady named Lorraine Henderson. I ended up dating her for many years. Lorraine had three beautiful children from a previous marriage. This worked out well for me because I did not have any biological children of my own, and Lorraine's children filled a void in my life. I am convinced that the Lord puts people in our lives for various reasons. I have been in their lives through their high school, college and raising their own children. I am fortunate to have Lorraine's children and now her seven grandchildren in my life. I feel as though they are my children and grandchil-dren because they have been in my life all of their lives. When people ask me how many children I have, I proudly say that I have four children and eight grandchildren.

After the 1988 Democratic National Convention in Atlanta, I made the decision to resign my position with the Democratic Party. Lorraine and I packed up the car and drove across country out West. I went out to Chinle, Arizona, to visit with my friend Milton Bluehouse, the Navajo Indian who I had met back in 1968 while we were touring Europe. We were gone for approximately two weeks. After I returned home from the trip, an assistant commissioner with the Department of Labor (DOL) asked me to talk to him before I made a decision regarding my employment.

In September 1988, I went to work with the Georgia Department of Labor as an assistant to the assistant commissioner. I was responsible for conducting fingerprint checks on new employees with the Department of Labor. I was also responsible for conducting workshops with all the employees on drugs in the workplace. I would go to every DOL office in Georgia to hold workshops on drugs in the work place. After I had been working with the DOL for approximately two years, the lieutenant governor, Zell Miller, asked the commissioner of the DOL, Joe Tanner, to allow me to take a leave of absence to come work with his campaign as he made his run for governor. Knowing how demanding the campaign trail can be, I still decided to take leave and join Zell's campaign staff. In fact, I looked forward to helping this great man lead Georgia.

Zell did not want to hire a white person to work specifically in the white community, and he did not want to hire a black person to work specifically in the black community. He wanted someone who had experience with working with both the white and black communities. The contacts that I made while working in the DA's office and the Democratic Party allowed me to establish contacts in the white community and what we call the "courthouse crowd," a term we use when referring to courthouse employees, especially in rural Georgia.

James Carville and Paul Begala were Zell's campaign managers and political strategists, and they did an exceptional job. They are both very smart, serious-minded and committed, but it was always fun working with them. I was working throughout the state of Georgia and no community or group was off limits. I was on the road almost every day and many times at night because some groups met at night.

We were forced into a runoff with Ambassador Andrew Young, who was Atlanta mayor, and Roy Barnes. We ultimately defeated Young and Barnes in the primary and then faced Johnny Isakson as the Republican candidate in the general election. Johnny had a lot of support from both Democrats and Republicans at the time. He had always been a moderate – even now in the U. S. Senate.

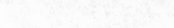

CHAPTER 20

GOING TO CAPITOL HILL

fter Zell won the governorship in November 6, 1990, I went back to the Department of Labor to resume my employment. Later, as Zell was putting his senior team together, he called me over for a meeting with him. In the meeting, he asked me to join his senior staff as his executive assistant for community relations. He told me that he did not want me to just handle minority affairs because he did not want to put me in a box. He wanted me to handle all affairs as they related to the governor's office, including those of blacks, whites, Hispanics, and everyone else.

Being selected as the governor's executive assistant was definitely another major milestone in my life. As I left his office that day, I could not help from thinking about my family, Father Joseph Cooney, Randolph Blackwell, Kenneth Goolsby, and others who had helped me along the way. I also thought about my earlier days of education back in that one-room school building where one teacher taught everyone from the first grade through the fourth grade at Level Hill Elementary School. That one-room school building, Level Hill Elementary, had propelled me to Capitol Hill.

I will be forever indebted to Governor Miller for having the confidence in me and giving me the opportunity to work with and serve the citizens of Georgia. I truly hope that I was able to make a difference in someone's life and help them along the way. My greatest reward came when I felt that I used the power of the governor's office to help others, especially the disenfranchised and downtrodden.

During his term, Governor Miller introduced and signed many significant bills into law. However, the most memorable one was the Georgia Lottery. I was intimately involved in the passage of the Lottery for Education Act, which would fund the HOPE scholarship. When Zell was lieutenant governor in 1988, he announced that he supported a lottery in Georgia that would fund education. A government-run lottery was unconstitutional in the state at that time. He was elected governor in 1990, and in January 1991, he introduced the lottery bill in the Georgia General Assembly while preparing to amend the State Constitution.

On January 31, 1991, the House passed the resolution to have voters decide on the lottery amendment, and the Senate passed it on February 8, 1991. The referendum was put on the ballot for voters to decide whether they wanted to change the State Constitution in order to a have lottery in Georgia. The passage of the resolution by the General Assembly was just half the battle. The other half of the battle was trying to convince the voters to support the lottery. The governor was hopeful that voters would support it because one-third of the funds would be used to fund college scholarships and other educational programs. The governor waged an all-out campaign for the passage of the referendum. He came to me and asked me to take a leave of absence from my duties at the governor's office to campaign for the lottery. I took a three-month leave.

Many churches and religious organizations opposed the lottery. I appeared on many radio talk shows along with persons who opposed having a lottery. People were very passionate about this issue both for and against. The governor laid out his plan for the lottery proceeds and how it would benefit Georgia students. He called it HOPE, which means Helping Outstanding Pupils Educationally. The proceeds were designed to be allocated to the following programs:

1. Scholarships for high school students who wanted to go to college or technical school
2. A pre-kindergarten program for 4-year-olds
3. Computers and technology for schools

After much debate and conversations about this issue, the voters finally had a chance to vote on November 3, 1992. The voters passed the lottery amendment, and on June 29, 1993, the lottery tickets were on sale in Georgia for the first time. (The first Cash Three numbers were 170.) Since the inception of the lottery in Georgia, many students and families have benefitted. I am happy to have been a part of such a successful venture.

There was another initiative put forth by Governor Miller that I am proud to have been involved in also. When we went in to office in 1990, Representative David Lucas from Macon, Georgia, brought statistical facts to us regarding the amount of business that the state was doing with small and minority businesses. Representative Lucas met with the governor and me to show how much money was being spent by each state agency with small and minority firms. The facts revealed that the state of Georgia was doing less than 1 percent of state business with small and minority firms.

In 1990, the state's budget was approximately $10 billion, and small and minority firms received less than $10 million of that. The governor told Representatives Lucas that this was "unacceptable," and he could be assured that the state would do better. As a result of that meeting, the governor issued an executive order directing all department heads and state agencies to do more business with small and minority firms.

The governor's Office of Small and Minority Businesses was housed in the Department of Administrative Services. The oversight of that office became my responsibility. I was responsible for assuring that these firms had an equal opportunity to do business with the state and had equal access to state contracts and bids. During the eight years of the Miller administration, an untold number of contracts and successful bids were awarded to minority firms than ever before.

The Department of Administrative Services records revealed that by the end of the Miller administration, the state had done more than $100 million in business with small and minority firms. I felt that this was still not enough, but it was a far cry from what it was when we went into office. If I had to rate my greatest accomplishments during my time in the governor's office, this would rate at the top.

CHAPTER 21
TRIP TO GERMANY

I n 1991, shortly after the Berlin Wall came down, Germany wanted to start their reunification process, bringing East and West Germany back together again. The German Consulate in Atlanta contacted Governor Miller and told him that its government wanted to invite a team from the United States to come to Germany to observe and advise the reunification process. They wanted people who were involved in government, banking, finance, business, and education. They wanted to get ideas, suggestions and perspective from a cross-section of people. The governor recommended me to participate in the three-week all-expense paid venture. The group was comprised of 23 professionals from all over the United States. We were able to offer, what I felt was, some useful recommendations. I am not sure whether they utilized our input, but I enjoyed collaborating with my colleagues.

We met at Rhenish Friedrich-Wilhelm University of Bonn (Bonn University). The university was established in the early 19th century and is regarded as an internationally renowned institution. We had the opportunity of touring and visiting many of the historic sites in Bonn. During the time we were there, we also had an opportunity to visit the Bundestag, which is the equivalent to our Congress. A very important discussion was going on in the Bundestag at that time. They were debating whether to move the capital of Germany from Bonn back to Berlin.

On the day that the final vote was taken on the capital relocation, we were in a local pub drinking beer with citizens of Bonn. As you might expect, tension was running high because Bonn residents feared that their city would become a ghost town if the capital were moved back to Berlin. With the voting process in progress, the German media was surveying individuals to get their opinion about the potential relocation. While we were sitting in an outdoor area of the pub having a beer, the news media came to our table with a camera rolling, asking us the question: Bonn or Berlin? I am not stupid, I thought. I was not about to say Berlin even if I felt that the capital should be moved there. All of us immediately said Bonn. The locals applauded our response, and they offered to buy us another beer. In reality, we did not care because it did not matter to us either way. After the final vote was taken, the decision was made to move the capital back to Berlin. We decided to go back to our rooms because the streets of Bonn got very rowdy, and we did not want to be caught up in the violence. The police was out in full force because the government suspected that there would be trouble.

After spending two weeks in Bonn, we moved to Berlin for another week of meetings and tours of the city's historic sites. Bonn was the seat of government, but Berlin was the economic engine that was driving Germany. It was touching when we visited remnants of the Berlin Wall that once separated Germany for 40 years into East and West Germany. A portion of that wall was still standing as a reminder of their history. Many people had lost their lives trying to escape from the East into the West. There were three major checkpoints to cross into West Berlin from East Berlin. The most notable one was "Checkpoint Charlie," which was closed in 1990. Checkpoint Charlie still remains as one of the most popular tourist sites in Berlin.

Visiting the place where the Potsdam Conference was held was equally interesting because I was a history and political science major in college. Therefore, I had read quite a bit about the conference to decide how to punish to the defeated Nazis. I really felt very close and connected to what I had studied because I was sitting in the same room that U.S. President Harry Truman, Joseph Stalin (Russia) and Winston Churchill (England) sat to discuss Germany's surrender in World War II and to divide up Europe. The conference lasted from July 17 through August 2, 1945.

The reunification of Germany presented many problems and concerns on both sides, the German Democratic Republic (GDR, or East Germany) and the Federal Republic of Germany (FRG, or West Germany). The East Germans felt as though they were second-class citizens. The professors who taught college in the East were kicked out because the communist doctrine that they had been teaching for 40 years was no longer welcome. The taxi cab drivers said they did not want to take fares into East Berlin because they could not find the houses because of the poorly marked houses addresses. Besides social attitudes, there were many more important issues they had to contend with during this process, including the monetary cost.

Ultimately, the reunification became more of an expansion of the Federal Republic.

This trip provided me with a better understanding of the history of Germany and how important Germany was to all of Europe. Meanwhile, I made many friends while visiting Germany. Our friendship has lasted for many years, and I am forever grateful for this.

CHAPTER 22
BILL CLINTON AND ZELL MILLER

Governor Zell Miller and Bill Clinton, the governor of Arkansas, were very good friends. Governor Clinton made the decision to run for president, and he solicited the help of his comrade. Zell wisely introduced James Carvill and Paul Begala to Bill Clinton because they were instrumental in his election for governor in 1990. James and Paul became household names in the campaign arena after the successful election of U.S.

Senator Harris Wofford in Pennsylvania and Zell Miller in Georgia. Governor Clinton hired James as his campaign manager and Paul as his chief strategist for his bid to become president of the United States. The Clinton campaign was run with precision even while overcoming many obstacles along the way.

Zell was instrumental in Bill Clinton's successful win of the Super Tuesday primary. His credibility was on the line in Georgia because he had gone out on a limb as one of Clinton's major supporters. Zell felt that if he could not carry Georgia for Clinton, then he would appear weak and vulnerable. Zell pulled out all of the stops, making sure that Clinton carried Georgia. Clinton's successful win in Georgia on Super Tuesday proved to be the difference that set him on a path to the white House. After Clinton was elected president, he was good to Georgia, for Zell had the ear of the president.

I was honored when President Clinton invited all of Zell's senior staff to the white House for a dinner and Christmas Party. As I was sitting in the white House with the president, I could not help from reflecting on where I came from in that little community of Level Hill in Crawfordville, Georgia. Going from Level Hill to the white House was a major accomplishment and a highlight for me. I will never forget where I came from. I remember what my mother said the day Governor Miller appointed me as his executive assistant. She said, "I am very proud of you and what you have been able to accomplish, but no matter how high you fly; you still have to come back down to the ground to get your food." My mother had a third grade education, but she was one of the smartest women I know. People in my mother's age group who lived in our area, spoke with lots of wisdom. They spoke in codes, leaving people to figure out the true meaning. I figured that out early in my life, so I was able to benefit from their insight throughout my life.

Being one of Governors Miller's executive assistants was a serious position with many challenges that came along with it. In May 1992, Rodney King's trial was going on out in California, and I had no reason to believe or feel that the verdict would impact me in Georgia. The evening the verdict was announced acquitting the white officers for the savage beating of Rodney King, small-scale protesters organized around the Capitol. When the staff got to the Capitol the next morning, we noticed trashcans that had been turned over and debris on the lawn.

The day after the verdict was announced, tension and unrest

had spread around the country and was starting to mount in Georgia. The students at the Atlanta University Center were gathering on campus to voice their feelings about the verdict. Keith Mason, our Chief of Staff, asked me to check with the presidents of the colleges in the Atlanta University Center to see if there was any sign of unrest brewing on the college campuses. I called and talked to all of the presidents, and they told me that their students had assembled on campus for a meeting to discuss the verdict and their displeasures with the justice system as it applied to black America. The presidents also told me that their activities were peaceful and confined to the campuses.

I went into Keith's office to tell him what the presidents had told me, and as I was talking to Keith, one of the secretaries came running into Keith's office. She said, "Frank, they are outside turning over your car." Zell was out the country on a trade mission, and he was on his way back while this unrest was occurring. Some students and street people came to the Capitol to protest their displeasure with the verdict and the justice system. At that time, we had limited security and police officers stationed in the vicinity or near enough to contain that crowd. We did not even have time to call in additional troopers or riot control teams.

All of the senior staff had assigned parking spaces on MLK Street on the east side of the Capitol. I owned a 1990 Blue Buick Park Avenue, and the other senior staff members all owned small or mid-sized cars. The protesters walked past the other senior staff members' cars and started rocking my car until they turned it over into the street. I went outside to see what was going on, and as I was walking toward my car, one reporter put a microphone in my face and asked, "Mr. Bates, how do you feel about them turning over your car?"

I thought to myself, "What a dumb question." I started to ask the reporter, "How do you think I feel? My car is upside down and possibly a total loss." However, I knew I had to give a politically correct response because I knew anything I said would be attributed to the governor.

Although I did not express my true feelings publicly, later on, I asked some of the protestors why they turned over my car, especially since I was the only senior staff member who was responsible for assuring that minorities had an equal opportunity to participate in state contracts. They told me that, first of all, they did not know that was my car. They thought that was the governor's car because of its color and size. They wanted to exact revenge, doing something destructive to anyone who represented government and authority. They understood that Zell did not have anything directly to do with the verdict. I understood their concerns, but I strongly disagreed with their tactics. I do not agree with the destruction of anyone's personal or private property for any reason. That verdict caused the city to be locked down for several days, not only in Atlanta but all over the country.

My brother, Howard, in Cincinnati, Ohio, was watching CNN News and saw me on TV. He called my mother in Crawfordville thinking that she had heard about the trouble with my car, but she did not know anything about it. Like I said, she was in Crawfordville, and she had not heard about what was going on in Atlanta or around the country.

I have never been one to question the decision of a jury. I may not like their decision, but I have learned not to question their decision or how they arrived at it. I was reluctant to call the unrest a riot because I spoke with a representative from the insurance commission's office, and they told me that insurance company may not pay if the claim grew out of a riot rather than an act of God. I told the governor not to call it a riot right then. "Let's wait until my insurance company pays my claim, and then you can call it anything you want," I suggested. The next day, I visited a white guy in the hospital who had been beaten for no reason other than just because he was white. His family was glad that I came to visit and reassure him that not every black person felt the same way. I kept in touch with him for many years after that visit. He is now living in North Georgia, still suffering from those head injuries. After many days of planning and meetings, things settled down and city, state and nation got back to a sense of normalcy.

In 1997, after having been in business with DUI schools for over 12 years, I made a critical mistake in judgment. I failed to report all the income from the DUI schools on my tax return. Once the Internal Revenue Service (IRS) contacted me about it, I kept the governor and our chief of staff abreast of the situation. I did not want the governor to be caught off guard just in case he got a question from a reporter. After several months of the investigation and interviews with the federal authorities, a federal grand jury indicted me for filing a false tax return on April 15, 1997. The governor was notified of the indictment after my attorney notified me. That same day, I informed the governor that I wanted to resign my position with his office. I knew I had made a mistake and I wanted to take full responsibility.

After several months of negotiations with a federal prosecutor, I entered a guilty plea. I knew that I had done wrong, so there was no need for a jury trial. As always, I stepped up to the plate and took full responsibility for my actions. The court sentenced me to five year's probation, 300 hours of community service, four months of house arrest, $3,500 in restitution, and a $1,000 fine. Shortly after I had completed all of my community service work, house arrest and paid my fine and restitution, I applied for a position with the Department of Technical and Adult Education (DTAE) with the Georgia Fatherhood Program. This was an ideal program because it gave me an opportunity to give back and help people who needed a second chance because I had been given a second chance. Many times, all a person wants is a second chance at life after making mistakes early on in their lives.

The Georgia Fatherhood Program was a program designed to assist and help noncustodial fathers to learn a skill so they could go to work and meet their child support obligations. This was a partnership between two state agencies, Department of Technical and Adult Education and the Department of Human Resources' Office of Child Support Services.

Many of the fathers really wanted to do the right thing, but many of them did not have the means to do it. Many of them had dropped out of school, had no GED, or criminal records, which made it difficult for them to find employment. At that time, Georgia had 36 freestanding technical colleges, and we had a fatherhood program at each of those colleges. The Office of Child Support Services would refer those individuals to me, and we would put them in our many short-term programs that had been developed just for them. We wanted to get them in and out as quickly as possible so they could go to work and start meeting their child support obligation.

Commissioner Michael Thurmond of the Georgia Department of Labor was another critical partner because his staff would assist those noncustodial parents in finding a job. This program served over 3,000 participants each year. We also had a companion program designed to help and assist the custodial parent as well. The Division of Family and Children Services (DFACS) would refer the custodial parent to our New Connections to Work program, and we would do the same for them: get them into short-term programs so they could learn a skill, go to work, and come off public assistance.

We had a New Connections to Work program at each of our colleges as well. Each year, this program served over 4,000 participants, who were mainly women (99%). As director over those two programs, I was proud of what we were able to accomplish and the many lives we touched. Many individuals who I do not even know would come up to me and say, "Thanks for giving me a second chance."

I would routinely reply, "No, thank you for giving me an opportunity to serve and give back."

On July 1, 2008, I retired from the Department of Technical and Adult Education with 31 years of service in state and local government. I will be forever grateful to those individuals who played a role in my life and helped me along the way. There are far too many to name or remember. My former boss Zell Miller would say, "If you ever see a turtle sitting on a fencepost, you know he didn't get there by himself. Somebody had to help him." Those words exemplify my life. I know that I am standing on the shoulders of many good men and women who scarified greatly for me and my well-being, and I will be forever indebted to them.

I am honored to have shared my life's journey from Level Hill to Capitol Hill.

(Top) Georgia Gov. Joe Frank Harris
(Left) My mother, Mary Bates, at the
Georgia Governor's Mansion in 1983
with Gov. Harris

Being sworn in as
Georgia Gov. Zell Miller's
executive assistant in
1992

Georgia Gov. Zell Miller's senior staff in 1997

President Bill Clinton and Hillary Clinton at a White House Christmas Party on Dec. 19, 1993

Me and "the boys," my classmates from Fort Valley State University

CPSIA information can be obtained
at www.ICGtesting.com
Printed in the USA
LVHW01s0047091117
555586LV00001B/23/P